the BOOK *of* **WHY** (AND HOW)

the BOOK of
WHY
(AND HOW)

DISCOVER *the* TIMELESS SECRETS
—TO—
MEANING, SUCCESS *and* ABUNDANCE

COREY POIRIER

NEW YORK

LONDON • NASHVILLE • MELBOURNE • VANCOUVER

the BOOK *of* **WHY** (AND HOW)
DISCOVER *the* TIMELESS SECRETS *to* MEANING, SUCCESS *and* ABUNDANCE

Published in New York, New York, by Morgan James Publishing. Morgan James is a trademark of Morgan James, LLC. www.MorganJamesPublishing.com

ISBN 978-1-64279-598-1 paperback
ISBN 978-1-64279-599-8 eBook
Library of Congress Control Number: 2019907958

Cover Design by:
Rachel Lopez
www.r2cdesign.com

Interior Design by:
Bonnie Bushman
The Whole Caboodle Graphic Design

Morgan James is a proud partner of Habitat for Humanity Peninsula and Greater Williamsburg. Partners in building since 2006.

Get involved today! Visit
www.MorganJamesBuilds.com

READ THIS FIRST

Download the audiobook *free.*

Just to say thanks for downloading or purchasing my book, I would like to give you the audiobook version 100 percent *free.*

To download the audio version, visit: www.thebookofwhyaudio.com.

Oh, and don't forget to visit www.coreypoirier.ca for more information.

DEDICATION

This book is dedicated to my seat-mate, Shelley, who has supported me in all of my projects and has made this book possible in so many ways.

I'd also like to dedicate it to my young, amazing son, Sebastian, who has already inspired me in ways I can't fully explain. I love you both so much.

And last but not least, thanks to my mother, Nancy, who has taught me what unconditional love truly means.

TABLE OF CONTENTS

FOREWORD

Corey Poirier is the perfect person to write this book.

He knows we live in a time when ever more people want to actualize their talents and dreams. And, not only has Corey followed his own creative path, but he has also fully digested the wisdom of the classic texts on the subject. He has interviewed over five thousand people who are also achieving their dreams, and he queried each one of them about "how" they did it.

If you find yourself reading his book, then you may sense that you, too, can break through to your goals.

In fact, I would argue that everyone can now tune into their greater possibilities as never before—because all we need to know about human growth and achievement is already in the world. Moreover, this information is now filtering out into simple steps available to anyone who wants to join the adventure.

What is this knowledge telling us? That we can individually bring into awareness what is most holding us back. I'm talking about those inner feelings telling us we may not have the ability to live our best lives, that only special people are destined to manifest their dreams, and that we many not qualify. Or worse, that we may have too many bad habits or emotional lows that would prevent such success.

These are the limiting thoughts that Corey thoroughly dispels with this book. Everyone, and I mean everyone, comes from nowhere to discover their life work. Anyone who has ever made a difference in the world has been inhibited for a time by doubt. So what? We now know how to maneuver ahead anyway.

The truth is, we all have a dream that we can bring into consciousness. It's, of course, not about becoming famous, although you never know. It's just about finding a place to make a difference. We can all systematically break through to a life that turns us on and allows us to find our special contribution to the world.

As Corey shows us, it is this feeling of personal calling that keeps us going. And I have to say, Corey's discussion about finding the "why" of our lives—Why find our dream? Why accomplish it?—is the most concise treatment of breaking through to our true purpose that I've seen anywhere.

Finding our true purpose is the wall-breaking key to finding our personal, creative happiness. And when we sense that what we want to do is helping the world in some way, we have the elation of identifying a need that is just waiting to be fulfilled. We catch the boost of energy that takes us beyond our perceived limits. And we begin to say, this is a task that needs doing! And, if not me, who else?

Helping the world for the better also sets us up for something more, something mystical, an unexplainable shift in luck or karma. Somehow as a result of our commitment to helping, suddenly we find that more people are entering our own lives to help *us*—often at just the right moment to reveal another step forward in *our* journey.

Imagine all this, and we've discussed only the first part of Corey's book.

After finding your why, Corey offers a second section that creatively guides you through the realities and competitions in the real world, giving you personal strategies that have proven successful for centuries.

And lest you think it is only a matter of hard work, Corey takes you through a third section that presents other mysteries that broaden your consciousness, feed your spirit, and help you become an even more fulfilled mentor of truth to others.

Being the accommodating fellow that he is, Corey gives you the option of skipping around in the three sections to find the ideas that best suit you. But I would say read the whole thing, every word, from cover to cover. Savor the energy of it in total. Immerse yourself in the gestalt coming from Corey's experience of being a master interviewer and absorber of creative knowledge.

Then step back and contemplate the complete experience of something we all want to do: rise above our perceived limits to live the inspired life.

—**James Redfield**, *New York Times* bestselling author of
The Celestine Prophecy series of books

PREFACE

Dreams. We all have the same doubts and fears.

Yet the tendency with most self-help books is for the reader to scan the manuscript for the highlights and then move on.

This movement toward breaking through to your best self and work has not only become a world-wide probability for ever more people, but the movement can now be seen as becoming conscious of itself.

We know, for instance, the roots and history of this awareness. I date it to the work of Dr. Carl Jung, who, amid professional ridicule, took the depth psychology of Sigmund Freud to greater heights. By stepping out on his own inspired track, Jung unleashed a wave of new pathfinders by establishing a new grounding for psychology in consciousness and inner spiritual discovery.

Abandoning Freud's idea that what held individuals back from their greatest fulfillment in life was not secret sexual urges but an existential fear caused by the superficial materialism and religious experience that had risen in modern society, he argued that the breakthrough point was to recognize that we could resolve our inner fears (and their other forms of expression in anger and the hurts we blame on others) by realizing that we are more than our ego thoughts about how to cope or pacify ourselves in a safe, limited life. Instead, he mapped out our ability to download an intuitive, higher spiritual guidance, fueled by inspiration and synchronicity, to reach our goals.

And that changed everything and opened the hundred years of advancement we have grown to call the human potential movement.

What we know is in this book.

MAKING THE MOST OF THIS BOOK

The book you are holding is the result of three years and thousands of hours of work. After gathering and including insights by close to five hundred thought leaders in the bonus portion of the book; researching, interviewing, writing; and working with my editor and formatter, this book may be my most labor-intensive work to date.

In the three Acts (sections) that make up the core of this book, my goal was to develop an all-inclusive text that could positively impact those just beginning their careers or businesses, those looking for a more meaningful way to operate a business or live their life, and those who want tangible strategies for taking things to a whole different level.

Act 1 covers the four *whys* that can change your life. Act 2 is about *thriving* in an all-consuming world, and Act 3 is dedicated to helping you become more *enlightened* as you move forward in life and/or business.

The book is broken down into Acts, like a movie or play. My hope is that as you progress through the Acts, you may experience similar progression to that of the hero or main character of a movie or play. The reason I am noting the Acts in this book is because I want to offer you a strategy for making the most of this book and respect your current learning desires.

Put simply, if you truly know your *why* already and know how to leverage your why to crush it on a daily basis, you will want to learn strategy for up-levelling your game. Therefore, you may want to skip to Act 2 and start there.

If you are crushing it at the highest level but are searching for more meaning, you may want to skip to Act 3, but if are looking to leverage your *why* while taking your game to another level and hoping to do it all with meaning, I highly recommend you start from the beginning and read in the order in which the book is laid out.

Worth noting, the book is also built in a way that the three separate acts are much like three separate books. You can literally spend time in one act and feel like you've completed a full book. To that end, there may be a story related in more than one place in the book, but only when the story adds value in both acts.

Oh, and if you want to learn/read exclusive insight from some of the world's greatest thought leaders—and I can't imagine you wouldn't—don't skip the bonus portion of the book where you'll find close to five hundred thought leader insights (quotes).

Don't forget to highlight and underline the heck out of this sucker. It was designed for just that. You can also access an exclusive bonus section, complete with exclusive videos, interviews, and more at www.coreypoirier.ca.

INTRODUCTION

A buddy of mine failed remedial typing and graduated high school only because his Canadian history professor gave him a final grade of 49+1 percent. He didn't read a book until he was twenty-seven, was a hypochondriac by age twenty, was hooked on energy drinks for more than two years, and didn't know the difference between fiction and non-fiction upon completion of high school.

Another buddy of mine became the youngest President's Club member in Toshiba Canada's history; launched the only of its kind personal/professional development radio show in a specific region; shared the bill with some of the world's most celebrated speakers; launched a business show that debuted at number two in marketing on the iTunes charts; launched a speaking podcast that has reached the top ten multiple times; interviewed everyone from Jack Canfield to Marianne Williamson; authored seven books in less than two years; spent time with Henry "the Fonz" Winkler, Hulk Hogan, and Deepak Chopra; broke bread with Dr. David Suzuki and the late Mr. Lahey (of *Trailer Park Boys* fame); spoke at multiple TEDx and MoMondays events; became the only Canadian-based coauthor for an international bestselling book released by twenty-seven coauthors; and shared the inspirational stories of thousands of individuals with thousands upon thousands of readers and audiences.

What do these two have in common? I am *both* of those dudes ("buddies").

Now, it may sound a little ego-driven to share the comparison, but here is why it matters. I have been on both sides of the fence, both thriving and struggling. I know how each side feels. I know it's not about money, achievements, or even the destination. Instead, it's about working to become the best version of yourself. The journey that results is its own reward.

As the great motivational speaker Jim Rohn said, "After you become a millionaire, you can give all of your money away because what's important is not the million dollars; what's important is the person you have become in the process of becoming a millionaire."

With over a million books released each year through publishers and over two million self-published books being released each year, you may ask, why another one, Corey?

I can honestly tell you that I wouldn't even put hands to keyboard if I didn't believe I could bring you something new. Your time is too valuable for another book with the same content.

Books, quite simply, changed my life. The first book I ever read was Dale Carnegie's *How to Win Friends and Influence People*. My mother picked it up at a flea market for twenty-five cents and offered it to me as reading material for a company retreat I was attending. Once I finished reading that first page, my life was changed forever. I was hooked.

The next book I read, *Think and Grow Rich* by Napoleon Hill, helped ensure that my reading days were just beginning. Both books played such an important role in my journey that I felt compelled, as long as I could bring something new to readers, to put together the book you are now reading.

To better explain my journey, I should note that since those early reading days, I've made it my mission to seek out and learn from the most impactful thought leaders I could secure time with. I had hopes that, much like Napoleon Hill years before me, I could gain a high level of exclusive insight to share with others. Here's the best part about what I discovered: achieving success, by any definition, doesn't have much at all (if anything) to do with your background, gender, social class at birth, or upbringing.

My journey has led me to meet some of the most successful and inspiring individuals in the world. I've learned their timeless secrets, those which truly allowed them to influence and impact so many.

Put simply, after interviewing more than five thousand thought leaders and practicing their wisdom for almost twenty years myself, I can all but guarantee that if you learn and follow through on practicing the principles I present, you will begin to see positive changes and achieve your goals more quickly.

These secrets have helped launch the highly successful *Chicken Soup for the Soul* series (over five hundred million copies sold as of this writing); helped people enjoy lifelong happiness and fulfillment; helped earn Grammy Awards; helped an individual become the twenty-fifth richest man in America; helped books like *The Monk Who Sold His Ferrari* exceed five million copies sold; launched the great Zig Ziglar empire; helped people go from little education to high-level success; taught people how to earn millions and change their financial blueprint in months (if not days); created highly successful acting, music, Olympic, and business careers, and so much more.

This book is part of my commitment to share what I've learned during this journey, and put simply, I feel people now, more than ever, need this exclusive insight. People are bombarded with information but struggle to find the wisdom that can change the game for them. This book is designed to reveal just that: game-changing wisdom learned during interviews with the best of the best.

Now, before we get into the meat of the book, here's an important question I'd be remiss not to ask: what would somebody who loves himself do? This is the question Hay House author Teal Swan regularly poses to her readers and viewers. When she shared this with me recently during a visit to Orlando, I realized almost immediately that somebody who loves himself would find new ways to grow and become the best version of himself.

I want to congratulate you for being that somebody. It's important to note that sometimes, when faced with new wisdom, we put on a hat I like to call the "I already knew that" hat. Undoubtedly, you may have heard some of what you're about to read. If that is the case, my simple request is that you try to find ways to tweak the parts you may know, put more of what you already know into practice, and explore the parts you haven't tried or heard before.

At seventy-one, Jack Canfield (*Chicken Soup for the Soul* co-founder and *Success Principles* author) has trained millions of people, yet he still attends seminars, takes notes, and then acts on what he has heard. This is certainly a beneficial attitude to embrace when it comes to learning and growing.

Consider this example from my good friend, elite skating coach Doug Shepherd. Doug has coached many NHL stars, including Sidney Crosby. When I asked Doug what he could teach somebody like Sidney, who already does 99 percent of it so well, Doug replied, "That's the thing, Corey. We're not looking to have Sidney change the 99 percent he is doing well; we're just looking for something in the remaining one percent that he can tweak that could result in perhaps an extra goal a game."

Even "Sid the Kid" and Jack Canfield, people who have essentially mastered their craft, don't wear their "I already knew that" hat when learning is at stake. My hope is that you won't wear yours either. My other hope is that you make this the book you read, then reread, and then recommend to a friend.

On that note, are you ready to make an impACT?

Act 1

WHY

Step 1

(DETERMINING YOUR) WHY

Find your purpose—your why—and you'll find your greatest way to make a difference.

—John C. Maxwell

I f you want to have as large of an impact as possible, you need to know your why. Your why is powerful—so powerful, in fact, it may be the only thing that keeps you from quitting when obstacles start piling up. Consider this common saying: "If you know your why, you'll figure out your how."

Simon Sinek's popular TED Talk "Start with Why" makes the case that all great companies know and start with their why, rather than focusing on their what. Since most great companies know their why, I feel it's imperative that individuals determine their why as well.

Social media influencer Bruce Van Horn discovered how true this was when he was diagnosed with cancer in 2014. Some would have taken the diagnosis as a reason to give up. In contrast, Bruce saw it as an opportunity to evaluate and focus on his why—namely, his two sons. Raising his two sons alone, he wanted to see them grow up and be there for them through their formative years. Those desires became his why.

Shortly after his diagnosis, he sat his sons down and explained what the diagnosis meant. Then, he announced that they were going to beat this thing and explained how they would beat it. The road they traveled from that point forward wasn't easy, but with determination and complete focus on his why, Bruce was able to win the battle. As a result of his desire to beat cancer and watch his two sons grow up, within one short year, Bruce went from lying in the hospital bed to running a full marathon.

This recovery and journey also spawned a top-rated iTunes podcast called *Life Is a Marathon,* which now impacts thousands of people each and every week. *Life Is a Marathon* is not a podcast about running; instead, the marathon is a metaphor for life. Bruce uses his show to share the stories of his guests, many of whom have faced heavy adversity during their journeys.

Bruce's book *Worry No More* became a bestseller. His Twitter account, with over four hundred thousand followers, allows him to positively impact even more people on a weekly basis. This impact was also part of Bruce's why, even if he didn't know it at the time. In fact, a lot of times during adversity, we discover new whys along the way.

As Napoleon Hill pointed out in his monumental work *Think and Grow Rich,* "One of the most common causes of failure is the habit of quitting when one is overtaken by temporary defeat."

I believe Bruce Van Horn's discovery of his why—and his ability to focus on it in the face of temporary defeat—was one of the things that kept him from giving up hope at a time it would have been easy to do so. Both Don Miguel Ruiz Jr. and Don Jose Ruiz have appeared on our show and talked about their passion and their whys. Together with their father, Don Miguel Ruiz, they have shared Toltec wisdom with the world through landmark books like *The Four Agreements, The Fifth Agreement,* and many more.

For the better part of the past thirty years, Don Miguel Ruiz Sr. has shared Toltec wisdom through practical concepts, with the goal of helping people transform their lives. His two sons, Miguel Jr. and Don Jose, have continued in their father's footsteps, even though they've travelled different paths.

In describing the importance of passion (their individual whys), each son had the following to say:

"Passion is the soul's creative force . . . When you find your passion, it's like the sun coming out. It's pure happiness."
—Don Jose Ruiz

"We may not control the world, but our work of art is our own life, and even if we don't control the world, we are the co-creators. For example, we can create an impact with a single word."
—Don Miguel Ruiz Jr.

The cool part is, even though all three took different paths, they arrived at the same why: sharing Toltec wisdom for the benefit of countless others.

Before we get to your why, how you can determine it, why you should bother, and so on, I'd like to share my why with you. My why is the combination of my passion, my purpose, my how (how I work with passion and serve my purpose), and the reason I was called to serve this destiny. I had to uncover my passion, determine my purpose, figure out how to serve that purpose, and figure out "why me" before I could fully determine my why.

In 1997, the only real business experience I had was running a small regional business newspaper that I had started eighteen months earlier. The business taught me more than I could have imagined, but the one thing it didn't teach me was how to thrive without cash flow. A year after I launched the regional business newspaper, I decided to close the doors. It wasn't an easy decision, and I was proud that I had been able to sell enough ad space (having never sold anything in my life) to keep the lights on for so long.

It was my first real career, and I was working on straight commission while also paying the business bills and my personal bills. (Interestingly, this newspaper had a big purpose in my life. I only discovered this later, mind you, but it was the reason I started interviewing business leaders, which is a major part of my life today.)

After closing the doors to my newspaper business, I accepted a position with Toshiba, the fifty-eighth-largest company in the world then. At the time, I only knew it was time to walk away from my newspaper business, and I also wanted to move across the country. My time with Toshiba eventually revealed the first catalyst behind my why.

I had no idea what kind of training would be offered at a Fortune 500 company and was surprised to discover the training was minimal. During my first week, I was handed a pile of blank business cards (and told to write my name on each), instructed to watch a Zig Ziglar training video, and directed to a boardroom to sit until further notice. There was no further notice—and no further training. Within days, I was sent out on sales calls and told that if I didn't produce sales results, any given month could be my last.

The Ziglar training video was transformational, but the lack of any inspiration or education directly from the company was disappointing. I didn't know it at the time, but this lack of training would lead me to decide to positively impact people who didn't receive the right training from their organizations. This decision was an important part of my why, even if it didn't seem so then.

The next step in my why was the discovery of my passion. I discovered my passion (or at least the door was opened) thanks to a series of bad nights on the stand-up comedy stage. I bombed for over a year on those stages before I finally realized my passion for speaking professionally. Nonetheless, discover it I did.

In Act 3 of this book, I speak about my purpose statement and the importance of writing your own purpose statement. Understanding my purpose (impacting lives in a positive way) means understanding my why—the two are essentially interchangeable. For those wondering how passion works into this, I define it as follows: passion is what you do, and purpose is why you do it.

So, my purpose statement (my why) now reads like this: I aim to be the guy who educates, donates, inspires, motivates, and entertains. It was everything to understand that my passion was professional speaking and my purpose was educating, donating, inspiring, motivating, and entertaining.

Next, I had to determine why I was the one to serve this purpose. Then, I had to take action. The "why me" part goes back to my desire to make sure as few as possible experienced the lack of training I had when joining or working with a company. I was fired up by the memory of what it felt like to be left to my own devices to survive, and then thrive, in one of the toughest industries I have ever seen. That fire would keep me going in an industry (professional speaking) in which I had no experience.

The second part of the "why me" came from my past experience. I had operated a newspaper where I had the chance to interview top leaders and gain exclusive insight I could share with others. I had also been performing stand-up comedy for over a year and gained unique insight about effectively communicating with others from the stage. Finally, I came from a business background that had offered me an opportunity to learn about communication, leadership, sales, and management.

The combination of my fire for teaching others, my ability to extract and share exclusive insights, the lessons I learned on stand-up stages, and my business background put me in the perfect position to work and live on purpose.

My why was born: to make sure every audience or person I spoke to was better for the experience and that they gained exclusive insight and wisdom they could use to become the best versions of themselves.

My *how* was through speaking and training from the stage and having one-on-one interactions with others. And so, I discovered my why once I:

1. Uncovered my passion
2. Decided on my purpose statement
3. Figured out "why me"
4. Determined "how"

Now, it's time for you to discover your why. In Act 3, I discuss passion and purpose in detail, even going so far as to help you create your own purpose statement. Since the first step to finding your why relates to finding your passion, I have included here the exercise I'll also share in Act 3 as I feel it belongs in both sections to make the book complete.

Excerpt from Act 3

You can find your passion at any age.

Why bother striving to find your passion? Well, when you have discovered your passion, you become excited to wake up and start each day; you can battle colds and flus more readily; you smile more; your heart sings; and people can't help but feed off your passion.

You can watch one of my videos to learn how to start the journey toward finding your own passion at www.coreypoirier.ca. Since this roughly seven-minute video gives you access to my strategy for finding your passion quickly, I'd like to shift my attention to purpose.

So what's the difference between passion and purpose? As noted above, they work together very well, and in fact, I use this formula to describe the result of combining the two:

PASSION + PURPOSE = SIGNIFICANCE
(profits and impact often result automatically)

From my perspective, also as noted above, the difference between the two is that passion is what you're doing (e.g., performing stand-up comedy), and purpose is why you're doing it (e.g., to entertain people and make them forget their troubles). I mentioned earlier that stand-up comedy turned out to be an extension of my true and real passion. It took a couple of years, but I ultimately discovered that my real passion is keynote speaking.

My real purpose is to inspire, motivate, educate, donate, and entertain through my speaking engagements. This is, in fact, my personal mission statement: to be the guy who inspires, motivates, educates, donates, and entertains.

Using a well-known example, Disney's purpose, as defined by Walt himself, was "to make people, especially children, happy." Perhaps realizing that adults are simply big children, Disney has changed its purpose in the years since. It is now simply "to make people happy." I believe that because Disney's cast members know their employer's purpose, they can serve in a way that continues to make the parks the "happiest place on earth." This is the power of knowing your why. It allows you to serve and make decisions that stay aligned with your purpose. It does the same for Disney and their employees.

So, let's shift the focus from Disney to you and discuss how you can find and work toward your why (also known as your purpose). First, you must discover your passion. The video above will help you, so don't skip that step.

Once you know your passion, then you can set out to create your own mission (purpose) statement. My belief is that once you know your passion, writing your mission/purpose statement becomes easier.

Why should you have a mission/purpose statement? Almost every successful company (even those you have worked for, perhaps) has a clearly defined mission statement, and I would argue it's even more important for each of us to have a personal mission statement. This holds true even more so for those of us who are self-employed.

So, let's begin. This exercise is really simple, albeit profound and very powerful. All you need to do is fill out the following statement:

My name is_____ . My passion is _____, and, therefore, my purpose is _____.

To make it easier, I'll give you an example: My name is Corey Poirier. My passion is speaking to audiences about passion, purpose, legacy, and customer service; therefore, my purpose is to educate, donate, inspire, motivate, and entertain.

This may take you some time, but if you can figure out and fill in this passion + purpose statement accurately, profits, productivity, fulfillment, and other benefits will soon follow.

Here's another demonstration of how powerful it can be to understand your why. Steve Jobs wanted Apple to be the company that was more than just computers. Harley-Davidson eventually realized they were a lifestyle company, not a motorcycle company, and they wanted to sell experiences rather than motorcycles.

Their whys? Apple wanted to be an innovative computer company that both put a personal computer on every desktop and offered people solutions they didn't even know they needed. Harley wanted to create lifestyle experiences rather than just sell motorcycles. These whys are so powerful that competitors (who mostly focus on *what* they do, not *why*) have essentially played second fiddle. I've mentioned Simon Sinek's TED Talk "Start with Why." Be sure to watch his video on YouTube to discover the why of these two industry giants in more detail.

So, now, the question is, what's your why?

Step 2

WHY NOT?
(THE QUESTION YOU MIGHT ASK)

You can, you should, and if you're brave enough to start, you will.
—Stephen King

I could actually start this section by asking you, what do you have to lose? During our interview with leadership guru Robin Sharma, he argued that many people die at twenty but don't get buried until they are eighty. "The walking dead," he calls them. These are the people who aren't living on purpose. If you're not living *your* purpose, you're probably living someone else's. From the last section, you already know you have everything to gain by discovering and living your purpose. So, why not step up and make your impact?

Consider the impact of Mark Goffeney, one of our former radio-show guests. Mark was born without arms. He came from a family with multiple children, and his parents raised him in the same way as their other boys. When he was still in his teens, Mark decided he wanted to learn to play guitar with his feet. Most people discouraged Mark, but that did little to dissuade him. Mark plowed forward. It took many hours, but sure enough, Mark found himself playing song after song with his feet. After that came bass guitar. Then, he took up singing.

Since that time, Mark has been involved with a video that was nominated for an Emmy, performed on stages across the world, busked in prestigious places like Balboa Park in his native San Diego, raised two children, done important work with Habitat for Humanity, and spoken at schools. Through media, his story has been shared countless times. You can watch videos displaying Mark's talent simply by typing Mark Goffeney in YouTube or Google.

Through his music, determination, and inspirational story, Mark has impacted more people than he'll ever realize. Imagine if Mark had said, "They are right; I can't play guitar," or "I don't have the ability to learn."

Consider author James Redfield. James has written multiple books. His first, *The Celestine Prophecy*, has sold over twenty million copies. The number of people impacted by his work is staggering. His work has changed countless lives. In fact, my girlfriend has said *The Celestine Prophecy* was the game changer in her life. James Redfield gave her a perspective she didn't know she had, and that started her on a journey she continues this very day.

James' work has impacted my life in much the same way. He has become a regular on our show and, dare I say, a dear friend. Imagine if James had said, "This work is too big for me. Someone else will have to pursue this project; I'm too busy not impacting lives." He may have had doubts, but without James Redfield, so many lives would not have been impacted in the same way.

Consider also Rick Hansen. Like his good friend Terry Fox, Rick didn't ask to be handed what some might consider a raw deal. At age fifteen, Rick was riding around and hanging out with some friends when he fell out of the back of the truck as it was accelerating. Rick sustained a spinal injury, and he was told he would likely never walk again. As a top athlete and possible future Olympian, Rick took this news hard. He told me that, many times that year, he asked the question, "Why me?" He struggled for a while and certainly didn't initially welcome the news he would not walk again.

In time, though, Rick Hansen embraced the cards he was dealt and went on to become a Canadian Paralympian, activist, and philanthropist for people with disabilities. He has inspired millions to reconsider what's possible. Through the fundraising and research efforts of the Rick Hansen Foundation, he is also playing a part in accelerating a cure for spinal cord injury and improving the quality of life for those with this injury.

In 1985, he launched his Man in Motion tour, which would see Rick wheel over forty thousand kilometers through thirty-four countries and four continents to raise awareness about the potential of people with disabilities. The tour ultimately raised twenty-six million dollars and became a catalyst for enormous change in the public's perception of people with disabilities.

Today, the wheelchair and many other items associated with the Man in Motion World Tour are preserved by the British Columbia Sports Hall of Fame and Museum. The song "St. Elmo's Fire (Man in Motion)" was written in his honor by Canadian record producer and composer David Foster and British musician John Parr, and it was performed by Parr for the soundtrack of the film *St. Elmo's Fire*. The song reached number one on the Billboard Hot 100 in the United States in September 1985. Imagine if Rick had said, "Why bother?"

The fact that you probably learned about this book online tells me you are in a better position to make an impact than millions around the world. Whether that impact is large or small is up to you. Any impact is better than finding reasons why you can't have an impact. Delete the excuses from your mind, determine your why (the previous section should help), determine the best action, and then take that action.

I want you to see there is truly no reason to prevent you from having a positive impact. In fact, let's think about some of the reasons "why not" that you may have used as excuses:

1. You're too busy.
2. You haven't found your why.
3. You don't have the energy.
4. You don't have the health.
5. You live in a small town.
6. Someone else will do it if you don't.
7. You don't have the resources or contacts.
8. You don't have the experience.
9. You're not happy with the way things are in your life.

10. You don't have the money.
11. You are afraid.

Ultimately, your biggest obstacle may be *fear*. If you want to make your own list, I'll still be here when you're done. Your list may or may not resemble mine, but in working with thousands of clients over the years, the reasons above are common.

Now that we have a reasonable list of reasons why you should not bother, let's examine each reason to determine if you should say, "Why not?" and then chase your purpose so you can have the kind of impact I know you're capable of.

Reason 1: You're Too Busy

You may be too busy because you have children to raise, work two jobs, or have a to-do list that's never-ending. These are valid reasons (and excuses). However, as I mentioned earlier, when your *why* is big enough, the *how* will work itself out.

Rather than simply rest on the laurels of that quote, let me give you some concrete examples. Consider my own life. I, too, felt (and still do at times) that I was too busy to live on purpose and have an impact. Everyone's "busy" is different, but I'd like to make the case that you, too, can find the time if your why is big enough.

My life today sees me operating a weekly radio show, delivering a "Learn to Speak" program, "Land your TEDx Talk" program, speaking on the road upwards of one hundred times a year (and some years as many as two hundred times), being interviewed by media outlets a few times a week, having a healthy relationship with my girlfriend, helping to take care of our son and three pets, practicing yoga and meditating weekly, watching Netflix (my guilty pleasure) multiple times a week, releasing twelve books (this is number twelve) since 2010, delivering multiple TEDx and MoMondays talks, and releasing my fourth music CD—complete with music video. And I still have free time left at the end of each week.

When I first said, "I'm too busy," I was only doing a tiny fraction of what I describe here, and I didn't feel I could take on more. Today, I am doing ten times what I was doing then, and I have time left over.

Every week, my show guests disprove the idea that there are not enough hours in the day. You might be saying, "Well, you're biased, Corey; you're trying to get me to make this change in my life."

I get that, so let me offer other examples to demonstrate there is enough time to crush your goals, live on purpose, and impact more lives. Take Arlene Dickinson. Arlene is an investor on the popular CBC *Dragons' Den* TV show. The show is basically the Canadian version of America's *Shark Tank* or, said differently, the Canadian version of the British TV series *Dragons' Den*. Another investor (at the time of this writing) on the show is *Shark Tank* star Kevin O'Leary.

The last time I spoke with Arlene, she was in the midst of raising four daughters (daughters she has raised mostly on her own), running the largest female-owned marketing firm in Canada, recording for and appearing on the hit show, speaking across North America, being interviewed by the media weekly, writing and releasing her first book, and traveling regularly. Yet, when I sat with Arlene, I would never have known she had any of that on the go. After two hours of chatting, I realized that I hadn't once heard her phone ring—I hadn't even seen her phone.

If Arlene can make time for an interview with my small publication, ignore the flurry of calls coming in, take care of her daily tasks, and still have free time, isn't it possible there is time for you to live on purpose and make your impact?

I could list person after person who is "too busy" to be living on purpose and making an impact but is doing so every single hour—in many cases, without so much as a single assistant. To name just one, Brendon Burchard, popular internet marketer, took his brand to a multimillion dollar level before he hired a single staff member.

Reason 2: You Haven't Found Your Why

This one is easy. I gave you the strategy in section 1 to get started.

Most people don't know their why when they first start. In fact, as I've detailed, many people live their whole lives without discovering it. But you now have a system for discovering yours, so let's just cross this one off the list.

Reasons 3 and 4: You Don't Have the Energy or Health

I'm not a doctor, so this shouldn't be considered as advice about health or a diagnosis. That said, I understand the complexities of health. Between the ages of eighteen and twenty-five, I was filled with anxiety, to the point where it transformed into hypochondria. (Hypochondria is the disease of thinking you have a disease when, in many cases, you don't, and it can include suffering the symptoms of each disease you think you have.) You may recall the scene in the movie *The Change Up,* when Jason Bateman explains hypochondria to his son. After hearing all of the symptoms, the boy replies, "That's what I have."

When you're a hypochondriac, you react with fear to every disease you hear about. You think, "That's what I have." During my battle with anxiety and hypochondria, I spent more time in waiting rooms than I did on my career—despite the fact I worked in a competitive sales industry that required many hours each week.

With my real and imaginary symptoms, my health reached an all-time low. Imagine the symptoms of the worst diseases. Then, picture your body taking you through those symptoms until your mind is convinced you no longer have that disease but a new one. Logic should tell you that you don't have the disease once the symptoms are replaced with new ones, but logic doesn't enter into a mind and body filled with anxiety.

I'm not trying to compare this feeling to actually having some of the terrible diseases I thought I had; I'm just trying to explain that I know what it means to feel like you don't have the energy or health to pursue your dreams. When I finally overcame hypochondria, I was diagnosed with hypoglycemia. With this condition, my blood sugar drops on its own, similar to the way it would with diabetes. It was a constant battle trying to get this in order—which is kind of ironic after battling so many imagined diseases.

Through this process, I discovered that living on purpose to make an impact and living my passion actually improved my health and restored my energy. As a result, I could begin exercising, practicing yoga, and meditating, which helped restore my health and body to what it once was.

Though I still prepare for the future, my fears of each imagined fatal disease convinced me to start living each day like it could be my last. Not having the energy or health to live out your why is a valid excuse, but, at the same time, it is the exact reason you should take steps to pursue passion and purpose.

Reason 5: You Live in a Small Town

This reason could have been valid in the 1980s—before the internet and efficient global travel—but it is not valid today. I live in a small town, the same small town in which I was born. I just moved back after living much of my life elsewhere, but I have achieved as much from small towns as from large cities, and that's mostly thanks to the connectivity of the world we now live in.

Consider Heather Moyse. Heather was born in Summerside, Prince Edward Island, the same small town where I was born. As we were growing up, Summerside had less than seventy five hundred residents. Yet Heather was able to spend much of her life in this small town and still become a two-time Olympic gold medalist, a successful motivational speaker, and a brand ambassador. In fact, many of the four thousand enlightened super-achievers I have interviewed were able to achieve success in small towns.

Dave Carroll, the writer of the song "United Breaks Guitars," was able to record his popular "United Breaks Guitars" video for less than two hundred dollars in a tiny town in Nova Scotia, Canada. The video has been seen by over fifteen million people, and his story has been heard by over one hundred million. In addition, the video and story launched a successful motivational speaking career that has taken Dave all over the world, eventually securing him a Hay House book deal. All of this happened without Dave leaving the small town in which he filmed and launched the now-viral video.

Regardless of where you live, you can achieve big things thanks to our small, global, connected world.

Reason 6: Someone Else Will Do It If You Don't

There is only one you. You have unique ideas and a one-of-a-kind life story. Other people might seem similar or have similar stories, but there is only one you.

The co-creators of the *Chicken Soup for the Soul* series, Jack Canfield and Mark Victor Hansen, faced over 140 rejections from publishers before one small publisher took a chance on them. The book series has since sold over five million copies.

How many others could have thought of the idea, come up with such a profound name, continued after so many rejections, and launched the series in the same way (Jack and Mark are known as master marketers)? It's perhaps safe to say *no one else* could have launched the same book series—a series that has inspired, motivated, and impacted millions upon millions.

There is only one Apple precisely because there was only one Steve Jobs (and only one Woz as well). Likewise, there would be another company competing with Disney on the same level if someone else could do it. But there isn't. There's only been one Walt Disney. There may be other directors running the organization today, but Walt needed to birth his unique vision in the first place.

The point? Since there is only one you, you have the ability to impact people in a way others can't—the world needs both your story and your impact. Don't make us miss out on your brilliance and creativity because someone else may (but probably won't) impact us in the way you could.

Reason 7: You Don't Have the Resources or Contacts

This is another valid reason, but again, not a deal breaker. Top networkers of today typically started with one thing in common: no contacts and no resources.

That was the case for author and speaker Harvey MacKay. When he wanted to convince a publisher to print one hundred thousand copies of his first book, he used an innovative strategy. He placed two briefcases on the table with each briefcase filled with over ten thousand business cards. He went card by card, listing how many employees each contact had. By doing this, he demonstrated he was serious and could sell the books that were printed.

The publisher had wanted to print five thousand and had never printed anywhere near one hundred thousand books for an unknown author. With his unique approach, Harvey persuaded the publisher to print the hundred thousand copies, and he sold those copies in record time. He had the contacts, and the publisher had the resources.

But do you know how Harvey built that Rolodex? One business card and contact at a time. He didn't inherit it, and he had no special skill that entitled him to twenty thousand contacts. He had gone out and built his network in the trenches.

A more recent example of this concept comes from John Lee Dumas. John is the founder and host of the popular *Entrepreneur on Fire* business podcast. When he launched his show, John was fresh out of the military and had absolutely zero presence on social media. John launched his show, one of the first of its kind, even though others said he was crazy to launch a daily podcast. His show grew, and then his social media presence and contacts grew. Today, John reaches millions with his show and thousands on social media, delivering his message and impact regularly.

The last time I checked in with John, his show was being heard by over one million unique listeners on a monthly basis and typically finishing in the top of the iTunes charts on a weekly basis. One million listeners for a podcast is a big deal. The fact that John was a virtual unknown when he launched his podcast makes his feat even more astounding.

Did I mention that John launched his show less than five years ago? Did I mention that John has been profiled in *Fortune* and *Success* magazines, received awards from iTunes for his charting history, and interviewed everyone from Tony Robbins to Gene Simmons? Yet five years ago, he had no contacts and very little in the way of resources.

I could go person by person with similar examples, but I think you get the idea. Most people who end up impacting lives in a big way started with few or no contacts—unless they had a well-connected family. But that scenario is less than one percent of people, I'm sure. Even Oprah probably started with no contacts, and she certainly started with very little in the way of resources.

Reason 8: You Don't Have the Experience

This has been the lifelong dilemma for many people. You need the experience to get the opportunity, and you need the opportunity to get the experience.

Here is the cool lesson I've learned: you get the experience by taking action and by doing. This means that the experience you're seeking is available, and no one else without the experience has a head start.

During my time in stand-up comedy, I performed in comedy clubs more than seven hundred times over the course of nine years. During my first show, I started without the mic turned on. I bombed show after show for the better part of three years before things started to feel like they were working for me on stage.

I didn't have the experience when I began, but instead of letting someone tell me I couldn't perform stand-up without experience, I found a comedy troupe that would let me fail while learning. That way, I could gain experience.

I went through a similar experience when I started playing guitar. I was tone deaf, didn't know any chords, and figured I'd quit before I could ever play a single song. Today, I have four CDs as well as songs on radio. I have toured, created a music video, and been nominated as a rock recording artist of the year. A similar thing happened with my speaking ability as well.

Now, you may be thinking, "That's all well and good, Corey, but I've heard that it takes ten thousand hours to master any skill." (This theory was made popular in Malcolm Gladwell's book *Outliers*.)

I agree that you can master almost any skill if you put in ten thousand hours, and I have tested this with multiple skills. But the good news is, you can shortcut that learning curve in most cases, and similar skills take less time to master once you master the first one.

So, how do you shortcut your learning curve? You seek out a person who has mastered the skill, and you convince them to mentor (or spend time with) you. They can teach you the shortcuts and show you the manholes they fell down so you don't fall down the same ones. Avoiding these manholes means shortening your learning curve because falling down and getting back out of the manhole often takes considerable time.

So, find a mentor, study what they do, ask them what they would do differently now that they have lived through their mistakes, and—even more ideal—put together a mastermind group made up of people who have achieved what you're trying to achieve and convince them to meet weekly so you can study and learn from them directly.

Multiple people who have achieved what you're looking to achieve can share wisdom that will help you reduce your practice by hours. This process won't replace active practice, but it certainly will shortcut the process.

To go one step further, "perfect practice" will help you cut even more of the hours you have to put in. The website www.bulletproofmusician.com describes the notion of perfect practice as follows:

"Perfect" practice is just another name for deliberate practice. Mistakes aren't the problem. The problem is not taking the time to articulate the specifics of the mistake, the cause of the mistake, and the potential solutions so you can avoid making that same mistake over and over.

Reason 9: You're Not Happy with the Way Things Are in Your Life

This excuse is actually the most pressing reason for taking action. And guess what? You're not alone. Most people, I believe, are not happy with their current lives. But you have the power to change your life and move away from the company of people not taking action. In fact, your decisions may be the only thing you can control.

My goal is to give you the reasons, motivation, strategies, and tools to change, but you have to make the decision to take the action. I certainly wasn't happy when I was battling anxiety. I know my girlfriend wasn't happy when she was battling an alcohol addiction. Alvin Law, a guest on our show, probably wasn't happy when he was being bullied at school because he was born without arms. Comedian Mike Bullard probably wasn't happy when he performed at a club where ninety-nine people out of one hundred showed up for the ninety-nine-cent spaghetti and just one person showed up for his act. I'm also sure that the person who drives on the highway ten hours a day wasn't happy the first time someone cut him off and flipped him the bird.

In all cases, though, we can decide to change our lives for the better. We don't have to stay unhappy. You can choose passion; you can choose purpose; you can choose happy; and you can choose how you respond to every "perceived" bad thing that happens to you.

For example, my girlfriend and I were in Memphis recently and decided to visit a museum that once acted as an underground railway house that hid slaves who were on the run. During the tour, the people working at the museum talked about the stories the slaves had told and the songs they had sung. As the tour leaders shared the stories of slaves who had all of the reason in the world to be bitter and unhappy, I realized that many had chosen humor and happiness despite misery and suffering. I believe they realized it would be easy to let the unhappy win, but they chose not to let that happen.

This reminded me of the story that Emilie Chiasson shared with me about her trip to Africa. She said the children she met were among the happiest people she had ever seen, despite the fact they didn't have running water or financial resources. They barely had roofs over their heads. It also reminded me about Mark Goffeney and how he decided to be happy despite being born without arms.

Make no mistake. You can choose to be happy. It may take writing in a gratitude journal each night; it may take surrounding yourself with positive (and happy) people; it may take faking it a bit until you make it. But you *can choose* to be happy.

I know because I did, and I have spoken to thousands of others who made the jump from unhappy to happy as well.

Reason 10: You Don't Have the Money
If *Shark Tank* has taught us anything, it's that you can get the money.

I was raised by a single mother, and money was so tight at times that we didn't have money for groceries.

Bill Bartmann was the richest person we've had on our show; he had been the twenty-fifth richest man in America. However, he didn't start with that money.

In fact, even having money won't help if you don't know how to keep it. Another show guest, T. Harv Eker talks frequently about a person's money blueprint. He explains that if you don't reset this blueprint and it's currently on spend, you'll have the same amount of money in your bank account five years from now as you do today. In many cases, this will be true regardless of how much you make in the interim. How many stories have we heard about people who win the lottery and, just a few years later, end up in the same place they started financially?

The point is, you don't need to start with the money, and it's more important how much you keep and invest than how much you start with. If you're truly living on purpose, you'll find the money. History has shown case after case of individuals who didn't start with any money but end up reaching the top level of their profession while living a fulfilling life following their passion.

Take Steve Jobs. Steve started with $1,350 (the proceeds from the sale of his Volkswagen) when he launched Apple from his garage with pal Steve Wozniak.

Arlene Dickinson arrived in Canada as a toddler with her father and mother. They didn't even have enough money to get to their intended destination, so they set up shop in a different city altogether. When she launched her business with other partners, they had to take a boat to a meeting (because they didn't have the money for flights) and combine their credit cards to stay in a hotel for a business deal. Today, Arlene runs the largest female-owned marketing company in Canada. She ultimately bought out all of her business partners, despite the fact she started the company as a single mother with absolutely no equity.

Colonel Sanders started Kentucky Fried Chicken with $87 he borrowed and raised additional funds by going door-to-door selling his chicken. Today, thanks in large part to the internet and affordable technology, you can start a business with literally no investment. Once you find your purpose, you can probably pursue it with minimal investment as well. You can even do things part-time while working on the side to pay for your passion. Countless Hollywood screenwriters and actors have done just that—worked, perhaps, as a cabbie by day and written throughout the night.

Reason 11: You Are Afraid

Tony Robbins has said that the key reason people don't take action is fear. I've heard many acronyms for the word fear. One of my favorites (or at least one of the funniest I've heard) is F**k Everything And Run. There is also the polar opposite one of Face Everything And Recover. The most common one I hear is False Evidence Appearing Real.

Here's the thing, though. For the person experiencing the fear, it is far too real.

Statistically speaking, the number one fear of the average person is speaking in public. That's why comedian Jerry Seinfeld has joked that, for most people, if they were at a funeral, they'd rather be inside the casket than doing the eulogy. It's common for someone speaking in public for the first time to shake visibly, sweat profusely, and, in some cases, pass out. Try telling that person their fear isn't real.

I'm not going to tell you your fears aren't real. What I am going to tell you, from first-hand experience, is that you can conquer your fears one small step at a time. Taking big steps and trying to conquer your fears in one big step is hard and very noticeable, but taking small steps and rewarding yourself for each step is a much surer way of facing and conquering your fears. In fact, if the steps are small enough and the rewards interesting enough, you may not even notice how close to your major fear you are getting.

In my research, I have discovered that almost everyone is yearning for growth. Facing your fears is a part of that growth. I have also discovered that your purpose and passion are often just outside your comfort zone.

Your fear may (or may not) be as real as you allow it to be. That said, you are more apt to discover the best version of yourself when you face your fears. Almost every influential leader we have had on our show had to face their fears to enjoy the life they now have. You can watch my TEDx Talk, How People Crush Fears and Expand Comfort Zones, where I discuss this in more detail on YouTube under Corey Poirier TEDx Talks.

In going through these eleven reasons why you shouldn't take a risk to step toward your purpose, I have provided proof there is actually no real reason why you can't move closer to making an impact.

Now, are you ready to take that step?

Step 3
WHY NOT YOU? (YOU MIGHT WONDER)

Your time is limited, so don't waste it living someone else's life. Don't be trapped by dogma—which is living with the results of other people's thinking. Don't let the noise of others' opinions drown out your own inner voice.
—Steve Jobs

In this book, you've heard story after story of people who had countless reasons not to, yet still decided to, find and live their purpose to make the kind of impact they were born to make. This is the reason I know you can also make an impact and are just the person to do it.

If you were born in a country where you have the freedom to pursue your dreams, you already have more advantages than many others who have made an impact. (Consider how difficult it must have been for Gandhi or Martin Luther King Jr. to start civil rights movements in India and the United States. Then consider what they were able to accomplish.)

If you have access to the internet, you already have more resources than they did. If you have all of your limbs, you are physically further ahead than many who have gone on to become bestselling authors, award-winning musicians, or sought-after speakers.

But as far as I'm concerned, the "why you" question relates more to what I've said earlier: the world needs *your story* and *your impact*. What's your story that the world needs to hear?

Let's answer some questions to determine why you are (or can be) just the person who can have the impact you were born to have:

1. What unique quality or ability do you have that sets you apart from others?
2. What do you think you could master in ten thousand hours?
3. What happened the last time you made someone smile, laugh, or become happy or inspired? If you can't remember, how could you make someone smile, laugh, or become happy or inspired?
4. What do people say you are good at (at home, the office, or when you're out with friends)?
5. What would your life look like if you were able to positively impact others on a regular basis?
6. If you really wanted to, what habit could you change, and how would that impact your life?
7. In the future, how would you regret never taking this leap of faith?

If Louise Hay could launch the self-help and new-thought publishing juggernaut Hay House at age sixty one and George Foreman could win the heavyweight championship at age forty-nine, and Martin Luther King Jr. could create a movement forcing society to acknowledge racial injustice and human rights inequalities through nonviolent activism, you also can be a person who impacts lives on a daily basis.

Remember, positively impacting lives can be as simple as offering to carry someone's groceries or lifting their luggage up to the overhead compartment on a plane—even just smiling at people as they pass could affect someone's day.

So, back to the question, why not you? The truth is, there is no reason why it shouldn't be you. You have everything you need (or access to everything you need) to make magic happen in your world. I know this because I have personally interviewed and spent time with thousands of people who are making small (and large) impacts daily.

You just have to believe it can be you. Far too many people have had their impact (whether business or personal impact) wiped out because they listened to the negativity of critics, friends, well-meaning family, or, worse still, themselves.

I would estimate that negativity (in the form of self-talk or comments from toxic people or even people who feel they have our best interests at heart) has been responsible for more loss of impact than anything else. Why do we take the words of critics so seriously? Many of these same critics don't have statues in their honor like Gretzky, Winfrey, or Lennon and McCartney have, and oftentimes, they haven't positively impacted as many lives.

I've had teachers tell me that I would never amount to anything; girlfriends tell me I had no business playing the guitar or singing in public; and friends tell me I was wasting my time operating my own business. I've had people tell me all of the reasons I couldn't do something that I later proved was possible. Other people have also shared with me all of the reasons life is supposedly against us all from the start.

I'm sure you've had your share of people telling you that you couldn't do this or that, that you couldn't have an impact or couldn't achieve a goal. They may have told you that throwing one starfish back couldn't make a difference, considering all of the starfish lining a beach. (The starfish reference comes from a fable where the man throwing the starfish back was told it wouldn't make a difference. He replied, "It made a difference for that one.")

Maybe you've already proved the critics wrong. Perhaps you need a reminder of how to deflect their otherwise "good intentions," or perhaps you want strategies to help you build immunity to those intentions. Perhaps you are wondering if you have a reinvention in you or if your best impact is behind you.

If that's the case, let me share that I recently sat down with Canadian music icon Bif Naked, who shared the experience of deciding to write her first book after an intense battle with cancer. Interestingly, she actually had little interest in writing a book in the first place and thought she did not have much of a story to share. The book came after years of success in the music industry, when it would have been easier to skip reinvention and just put out another great rock album. Yet, her comment after going through the experience is significant: "I now know that reinventing yourself in your 30s, 40s, 50s, and beyond is totally possible."

So, whether you're just starting your journey, starting a new journey, looking for a reminder about how to overcome the obstacles standing in your way, or looking to reinvent yourself, one thing is certain based on my research: regardless of what you have told yourself or others have told you, it is possible.

Do you need a further answer to the question, why not you? The truth is, it *has to be you*. No one else can have your impact. As Jack Canfield noted in his book *The Success Principles*, "You can't hire someone else to do your push-ups for you."

If you don't take action and are filled with regret later, you can't blame someone else for taking that action instead of you. If someone else ends up reaping your happiness, impacting lives you could have impacted, or making the difference you wanted to make, there is no room for complaining.

Perhaps it's time to consider what you want to achieve and start making plans for the actions you could take in that direction. Start believing it is within you to be the person who enjoys the impact you can create. You get to choose what that impact is—whether it involves opening a specific business, heading a certain cause, helping a person each day, or some other endeavor. You simply must have faith that you can do it. As Deepak Chopra notes, "You must find a place within yourself where nothing is impossible."

This may be a good time to help you determine all of the things you can do (no matter how small or large) so you can see how much you can accomplish. My hope is that I have convinced you there is no good reason that you can't be the one to have the impact you were destined to have. I hope you now believe it to be true.

Here is another thing that is true: it is much easier for you to believe you can do it and/or succeed in doing it (whatever it may be) if you have a solid strategy in place for deflecting negative influence and embracing positive influence. Make sure to check out the strategies provided at the end of step 5.

WHY NOT NOW?
(RATHER THAN TOMORROW)

The best time to plant a tree was twenty years ago. The next best time is now.
—Proverb

We now know your why, and we know that you have nothing to lose and everything to gain. We know that it can and should be you. But why is *now* the right time?

First of all, today is better than tomorrow because even now someone is already waiting for you to impact their life in a positive way. To continue the proverb theme, there is a great German proverb that reads, "One today is better than ten tomorrows." There is also the familiar saying most of us have heard: "Why put off until tomorrow what you can do today?"

To me, it simply comes down to this: no one is guaranteed a tomorrow (or a full twenty-four hours today, for that matter). So, if someone is waiting for your positive impact, you may not be around tomorrow to deliver. In my experience, few things feel better than positively impacting your own life and the lives of others in the process. Why would you want to put off that experience until later when you can experience it now?

There has never been a better time or greater need for your personal or professional impact than now. For example, look at the division resulting from the American election. What has this rift shown us? There have never been more people openly looking for hope or openly looking for change. What if you can provide that hope or change? Maybe you can provide both.

If you know how you deliver value to others and you take action, I think you'll find the timing is not just right—it's perfect. Remember, when people are looking for hope or change, it could simply be the act of showing you care about them that gives them faith in humanity.

In addition to being the right time because of what is happening in the world and how the world is feeling, there has never been a better time in terms of logistics and reach. For the first time in history, individuals and small businesses can have a similar impact to that of a large business or people with large followings. Developments like social media have made the world much smaller, and it's easy now for people to build tribes. Technology is allowing us to reach others in new ways and accomplish more than ever before.

Consider Bruce Van Horn, whom I've mentioned. Without being a celebrity, Bruce has built a group of close to five hundred thousand followers on Twitter alone. Another recent show guest, Ami James, of *Miami Ink* fame, has more than three hundred thousand followers on Twitter, close to four million on Facebook, and more than five hundred thousand on Instagram. His new Facebook Live show reaches over one million viewers each week. Cameron Dallas, star of the Netflix show *Chasing Cameron,* has over seventeen million followers on Facebook.

I could list individual after individual who just five years ago didn't have a massive influence yet now could sink a business or positively impact millions of lives with a single post.

In the past, you had to have a global company or unique access to the broadcast media for that to be possible. Ami James has been off network TV for quite some time, but he was able to create a Facebook Live show for over a million viewers weekly without any experience in the Facebook Live medium beforehand.

Whether your goal is to have the kind of impact Bruce, Ami, or Cameron are having or to simply inspire a person each day, there has never been a better time to do so. If your goal is to reach the level of influence these influencers enjoy, you may be thinking, "Did I miss my opportunity, or will I need to put in years of effort to achieve that kind of influence?"

Here's proof of what's still possible: social media influencer Simonetta Lein shared with us recently that the majority of her following (more than three hundred thousand on Twitter, 183,000 on Instagram, and more than one hundred thousand on Facebook) was built in less than six months. That's more than five hundred thousand people she can impact daily.

When we asked for her secrets for building a similar following (and, therefore, similar influence and impact), she noted it comes down to these tips:

1. Offer a different perspective on what it is you do (i.e., your why).
2. Be consistent with your messaging.
3. Help other people online and engage with them (rather than just talk to them).
4. Deliver value for others.

Notice a theme that is similar to what we have just shared about how to have a business impact?

If I had a great cause and wanted to reach a lot of people in a big way, our radio show guests (many of whom have since become friends) and others within my network could, in theory, collectively reach well over a billion people.

How did I build a network that allows me to have such an impact? I simply tried to stay true to my why while helping solve problems for others and continuing to give and give and give. Hmmm, this is becoming a common theme, isn't it? Hopefully, this makes the case as to why now is the time.

With people desperately looking for change and hope and with what is possible today in terms of reach, there are certainly more ways than ever to impact people. I hope I have convinced you that, regardless of the economic conditions now or in the future, there has never been a better time for you to stand up and make your impact. Let's give you another reason why now is the greatest time to make your mark: distraction. Just about everyone is more distracted than ever.

We had a doctor on our show, and she spoke about the fact that each time we receive a message on our phone, we get a shot of dopamine/endorphins. It's basically like getting a natural high. I've heard about many a study that has proven this, and even at my most recent TEDx Talk event, two of the other speakers cited studies on this as well.

What does it mean? Well, it means that our affection for our phones is not just a habit; it is an addiction. Imagine, though, if you were one of the few who could remain focused, one of the few who could go all in with the people in front of you—only giving your full attention to your phone at the appropriate time. Wouldn't that put you in a better position than those who can't fully connect with others while near their phones or in a better position than those who are always distracted?

To me, this ability to focus gives you a distinct advantage to accomplish more and have a deeper impact. It means exhibiting willpower over modern distractions, but I believe it's worth it. It makes it a great time for you to make your mark.

It's not just the phones that distract. It's the noise on social media, the billboards we see each day, television, and so on. Regardless of the distraction, the situation is the same. If you can turn off the distractions and go all in on each thing you are doing at any given moment (and be present), you will be able to have a bigger impact than if you are distracted over and over throughout the day.

Again, I feel this makes now the perfect time for you to take action.

Even if the economy is on the downturn, consider that amazing brands and empires (Tony Hawk, Coca-Cola, the Oprah brand) were either built during a recession or continued to thrive during a recession—so even the economy shouldn't halt your ability to make your mark today.

Whether it's more people looking for change or hope, our world becoming so much smaller thanks to technology and social media, or everyone walking around distracted, you have a great opportunity to play a bigger part. Now is truly your time.

Even though I've delivered on the four whys we focused on in this book, before I let you run off to make that mark, let's consider how you could create an Invisible Impact (positive ripple), and then deliver some *hows*.

Step 5

CREATING YOUR INVISIBLE IMPACT

If you think you are too small to have an impact, try going to bed with a mosquito (in the room).

—Anita Roddick

I was recently speaking with semi-retired public relations specialist Bill Vigars. Bill was the public relations person for Terry Fox's Marathon of Hope. Terry Fox was a cancer research activist, Canadian athlete, and humanitarian who had his leg amputated but decided to run across Canada to raise awareness about cancer and the importance of cancer research. He ran twenty-six miles each day until he was forced to stop just outside of Thunder Bay, Ontario, after his primary cancer spread to his lungs. He had completed 143 days and 3,339 miles (5,373 km). Bill shared that Terry was weary of the word "hero," fearing that as people embraced him as a hero, they forgot about cancer.

Bill also shared that Terry realized that being forced to stop his run early would remind people about the importance of finding a cure for cancer. Terry Fox knew he wouldn't live to see that cure, but he was passionate about playing a part in raising as much awareness as he could.

By the end of his run, Terry was embraced by the media and the country. What many didn't know was that his tour started out quite differently. In the beginning, Terry and his friend Doug started making their way across the country in a small van. Terry ran twenty-six miles (forty-two km) each day and then slept in the cramped van, which also contained their small bathroom and stove. The pair enjoyed no fireworks, no confetti, no big media buzz, but part of Fox's inspiration came from the small number of individuals who approached him during his run to tell him that his work wasn't going unnoticed.

Since that time, more than thirty-five years ago, Terry Fox has become a symbol of inspiration, and his name has helped raise upwards of seven hundred million dollars in the name of cancer research. People continue to raise funds. Students today, who were not born during Terry's Marathon of Hope, run in his name and honor.

Terry Fox has had a massive Invisible Impact. But it all started with two guys in a van and an idea to raise funds for something they were passionate about. I've mentioned other Invisible Impact stories later in this book (the Jimi Hendrix story, Mark Goffeney's story) and mentioned that your action doesn't have to be grandiose to make a difference. It can be as small as a smile at the right person at the right time. I hope you will decide to take some action, any action, toward creating your own Invisible Impact.

To end this short section on impact properly, I want to give you a crucial component I have discovered for creating and having an Invisible Impact (big or small). I hope it will help you start a positive ripple in your world. Here you go: it is important to serve, love, and care (for altruistic reasons) if you want to have a positive impact.

I recently interviewed *Chicken Soup* co-creator Mark Victor Hansen. He noted that entrepreneurs have a unique opportunity to "serve for the sake of serving, love for the sake of loving, and care for the sake of caring." I believe this is the key to having the Invisible Impact you can and want to have.

A couple of years ago, I interviewed seasoned networker and politician Matt Whitman. When I asked him about the importance of giving back, he recalled the moment that changed his life and behavior for the better. That moment was the day he realized that he had spent the first twenty years of his life focused on himself but wanted to spend the next twenty years (and the rest of his life, in fact) focused on others.

He added a quote that a friend of his had shared with him years earlier: "If you want more love, give more love." In this quotation, we can change the main word (love) to almost any area of our life, and it still applies. For instance, "If you want more hugs, give more hugs"; "If you want more peace, give more peace." And, on the other side, "If you want more hate, give more hate."

The message is clear: Matt has discovered that giving brings him much more joy (and, dare I say, purpose) than taking.

On our radio show, we regularly talk with enlightened super-achievers about the importance and power of being of service to others. Not surprisingly, the vast majority of our guests believe in the power of giving back and being of service, and they spend a large majority of their time doing so.

These super-achievers also believe that serving others enhances their own well-being and provides optimal levels of happiness—even though they are often making a difference in the lives of many others in the process.

If you can figure out how you were meant to serve for the sake of serving, love for the sake of loving, and care for the sake of caring, you will not only create a powerful Invisible Impact (regardless of the grandiosity of your actions), you will also have amazing potential to improve your own well-being and optimize your own level of happiness. Not a bad pay-off for doing what feels right in the first place.

Step 6

HOW (CAN YOU TAKE **ACT**ION)?

Even if you're on the right track, you'll get run over if you just sit there.
—Will Rogers

A s promised, after all of the *why* talk, here are some strategies to help you take action and get past the negative talk and influences that may be holding you back. (Warning: Applying these strategies will likely bring more positivity into your life and convince you that it should be *you* who takes action.)

Strategies for Reducing or Eliminating Negative Self-Talk

Gratitude

If you want to reduce negative self-talk, a good place to start is realizing how much you have going for you and how much you have to be thankful for. One of our past interviewees, inspirational speaker Candace Carnahan, lost her leg in a workplace safety accident. She shared with me about times when she realized how much she had to be grateful for, including once when she was running down the street on a new artificial leg that was hurting her. On the side of the road, she saw a person watching from a wheelchair. She quickly realized that individual would be happy to have a sore leg if he could get up and run down the street.

What do you have to be grateful for? I bet if you started a gratitude journal (if you don't have one already) and wrote down just five things a night (even one would be a start), you would be amazed at just how much you have going for you. If you kept up this practice, in time, you would witness your negative self-talk become a thing of the past.

ACTion: Buy a journal and daily list all you are grateful for.

Reframing and Perspective

My mother and I were in a coffee shop drive-thru recently, and the gentleman behind us began yelling out of his window for us to hurry up; he complained that he was just ordering a coffee, and we were holding up the line. It was Mother's Day, and my mother didn't hear him yelling, but I told her about it once we were a mile or so down the road. She immediately got upset. "Let's go back there; I want to have a talk with him," she said. I suggested it was possible that he had lost his mother on Mother's Day or that he didn't get along with his mother and Mother's Day reminded him, so he had taken it out on us, a mother and son in a car together. Once I offered that perspective, my mother's tone softened. "Awww, that's probably what's going on," she said. "Let's go back and pay for his coffee."

If you can reframe your perspective on a situation, I believe you can change your outer and inner talk.

E + R = O (Event + Response = Outcome)

When you begin to talk negatively about or to yourself, that is the event in the above equation. You'll have a hard time controlling exterior events that occur—be they related to the economy, an election, or some other happening—but you can absolutely decide on your response. The response you choose will ultimately determine the outcome you experience.

As the great quote says, "Life is 10 percent what happens to you and 90 percent how you react."

To reframe an event or to consider a new perspective on the event now in front of you (including negative self-talk), take a breath. Most people react quickly without thinking. As a result, they react based on emotion, instead of thinking and then responding with a logical choice. If you take some time (even just seconds) to consider the best response, I think you'll find you can choose a more positive way to respond to the event and reframe your perspective. Taking this action will help you recondition yourself to become a positive self-talker.

If you want a great example of how your response can have a profound impact on the outcome of an event you face, consider the story of Patrick Henry Hughes. Patrick was born without eyes, and he cannot bend his arms and legs fully. People have said to me after hearing his story, "Man, he was delivered a raw deal." Patrick sees it differently.

During our interview, I asked Patrick if being born with a perceived disability made it difficult for him to achieve at the level he has. He immediately responded that he actually feels he was born with an ability that people with sight don't have. He continued that people with sight often judge the people by what they see on the outside (i.e., by their background, clothes, color of their skin) whereas he actually judges people by what they are inside. He feels this is an ability many don't have.

I believe Patrick's perspective is the biggest reason he has enjoyed the life he has. Patrick has impacted millions of lives with his story. He has appeared on *Oprah* and *Extreme Makeover*, released a book called *I Am Potential*, spoken to audiences across North America, and graduated with honors from the University of Louisville while also playing in the marching band. In short, he doesn't seem to lack in many areas.

His is a classic example of responding positively to an event so that his outcome could be far better than if he responded negatively. In this case, the event was being born without eyes and with physical ailments. His response was to consider these conditions as gifts, and the outcome is that his life has delivered many, many blessings while positively inspiring others.

ACTion: Think about the last three events you encountered and how you responded. Consider if a different response would have led to a different outcome.

Now, let's talk about strategy to help you get past the negative people or influences that may be holding you back.

Strategies for Reducing the Effect of Toxic People or Influences

Surround Yourself with the Right People (an Exercise)

In 1997, I was battling anxiety in a big way. That battle continued for years, but by 2002, after discovering my passion, I found that my symptoms and much of the struggle had all but disappeared. A few years later, the struggle began to return. I couldn't figure it out. My life had transformed, yet it felt like I was starting to go backwards.

I decided to do some deeper work to figure out what was influencing my thoughts and behaviors, to see if something had changed. One of the exercises I created involved determining if the people with whom I was spending my time were having mostly positive or negative influences on me.

The exercise involved simply taking a pen and a piece of paper and drawing a line down the center. On one side of the line, I noted people who were bringing mostly positive energy to my life (i.e., they didn't gossip much; they inspired me; they didn't tell me all of the reasons I couldn't achieve this or that). On the other side, I listed people who were bringing mostly negative energy (i.e., they gossiped often, mostly spent their time in the doom-and-gloom universe, and tried to tell me all of the reasons I couldn't achieve this or that).

Listing the negative-energy people on one side and the positive-energy people on the other helped me see what kind of people I was surrounding myself with. I was absolutely shocked to see that out of the eighteen people on my list, more than half were bringing me negative energy.

Before actually doing the exercise, I would have bet my list would contain more like sixteen positive and just a couple of negative people. Here is something I have learned many times over: if you have a greater negative than positive influence in your life, you are going to have to work much harder to bring yourself out of funks or deflect negative energy than if you have mostly positive people influencing in your life.

Once I knew the numbers, I was easily able to determine the people I wanted to remove from my life, the people I wanted to spend less time with (e.g., a family member I love greatly and wouldn't remove but would decide to limit his influence), and the people I wanted to add to my life or spend more time with.

Practicing this exercise and taking action not only greatly improved my life and helped fend off anxiety, but it also positively impacted my personal and professional performance.

Have you ever actually looked at who is in your life and what kind of impact they are having? Here is a grid so that you can try the same exercise for yourself:

People Who Add Positivity	People Who Add Negativity

Add the totals of positives and negatives. If you have more negative people in your life than positive, you might have some work to do.

Feed Your Mind the Right Things

In interviewing so many enlightened thought leaders since 1996, I can tell you with certainty that the second-most common trait they share is the habit of lifelong learning. As the late Zig Ziglar argued, such people realize that even though they may finish school, they should never decide to finish educating themselves.

Whether it be wrestling hall of famer Jake "the Snake" Roberts studying the wrestling tapes of the wrestling legends or former *Success* magazine publisher Darren Hardy continuing to interview many of the world's top thought leaders so he can gain exclusive insight, interview guest after interview guest has shared with me how they continue to feed their minds.

I heard about a Charles Schwab study some years back that discovered that the top two percent of North American CEOs clearly had something in common: they all read between three and five of the right books per month. The same study showed that the average North American read less than a half of a chapter per year, if memory serves me.

It's perhaps also no surprise that the thought leaders of yesteryear (Henry Ford, Thomas Edison, Dale Carnegie, Ralph Waldo Emerson) all had personal libraries, even though many of these leaders didn't complete high school. In fact, when we visited Concord, Massachusetts, a few years back on our Invisible Impact Tour, we saw Ralph Waldo Emerson's personal library. Wow! I expect it could rival many small public libraries of the time.

When we interviewed Zig Ziglar before his passing a few years back, he shared that at that stage in his life, he only read biographies, self-help books, and inspirational true stories because he felt those were the key books that could allow him to continue growing.

We had another interviewee share with us that she decided what to read by asking the people she admired what they were reading. When a title came up multiple times, that was what she read first.

There are some great hints in here. First of all, if you want to be a thought leader who makes a big impact, you should feed your mind the way top leaders do. Second, read or feed your mind the type of wisdom that will help you expand your mind in the most efficient way. Find out what top leaders are using to feed their minds and feed your mind with those items first.

Here's some great news. In the past, you almost had to be a reader or enjoy reading to feed your mind. Not today. With TED Talks, podcasts, audio books, niche online TV shows, YouTube, social media, and other sources, you no longer have to be a reader to feed your mind efficiently.

In fact, I have many clients who have taken to my idea of putting together a TED Club (rather than a traditional book club) so their staff can watch a specific TED Talk and then discuss it at staff meetings. I am just about to incorporate this idea into my current Mastermind, and I also recommend that others incorporate it into their lives as well—even if it's just you and one other person watching the same TED Talk and discussing it (like my girlfriend and I do as part of our TED Tuesdays ritual).

To the best of my knowledge, speaker Brian Tracy coined the term "mobile library" when he noted that many people are driving in their cars for hours each day; in essence, they could almost gain the equivalent of a university degree while driving to and from work if they chose to listen to the right things. Brian is simply suggesting that you are already in the car, so why not use that time to feed your mind?

Another of our former interviewees suggests a learning approach that I use to this day. He calls it his "hour of power" and credits it for much of his success. Jack Canfield, co-creator of *Chicken Soup for the Soul*, dedicates the first hour of his day to three twenty-minute habits: 1) exercising 2) learning and 3) mindfulness. Here is what he says about this practice:

> "Almost everyone in North America is watching three to six hours of television a day, and if you cut that by just one hour per day, that's like nine-and-a-half work weeks, or two months. If we just take that hour a day and devote it to education and health and inner peace . . . People always ask me what's my secret to success, and I say it's that I'm always learning, and I'm always meditating . . . That one hour can transform your entire life."

Many people tell me they can't fit another hour into their lives or they don't have time for feeding their minds, exercising, or sitting in stillness. At first, I thought the same, but I want to share an example of how easy it is to fit this into your life without feeling like you're taking on something else.

This can work for you even if you don't go to bed an hour later, get up an hour earlier, or replace TV watching with something else (although I think each of these options could serve most people well). I'm a big believer in accomplishing multiple things with a single effort. This is probably why I love the book *PUSH,* written by one of our past guests, Chalene Johnson of Turbo Jam.

In the book, she talks about focusing on the goals that will mean crushing multiple goals with one effort. For instance, writing a book could mean becoming an expert, launching a speaking career, getting into other doors that may not be open without the book, or opening up another revenue stream (and perhaps passive revenue). Getting more fit could mean sleeping better, accomplishing more each day, having more energy, meeting new people, and so on.

I decided to use the same concept to bring Jack's "hour of power" into my life. For example, I have to walk our dog, Sprocket, each morning. I realized I could accomplish the exercise portion of my hour of power while I'm walking him. I am a bath guy, so I typically take a bath first thing each morning. I can listen to a guided meditation or sit in stillness while also soaking in my bath. If I'm taking a shower that day, I can stay in bed ten minutes longer but stay awake and listen to a guided meditation then. This way, I'm covering the stillness portion of my "hour of power."

Finally, for the feeding of my mind, I can watch a TEDx Talk (which takes less than twenty minutes) before I jump into my day. Another option is to read an article or two in *Success* magazine with breakfast.

Many days, I'm driving to or from somewhere, so I can listen to an audio program during that time. In fact, if I really wanted to combine activities for maximum time efficiency, I could listen to a podcast while walking the dog in the morning and, therefore, cover two of my three "hour of power" items at once.

Whether you decide to read the right books, watch and discuss a TED Talk, listen to audio while driving (or walking or running) each day, amass a personal library to match that of Emerson's, or dedicate the first hour of your day to learning, exercising, and mindfulness, simply know that if you want to have a positive impact, you need to feed your mind with positive things.

Limit the News

My mother was diagnosed with cancer more than twelve years ago. At the end of her meeting with her doctor, he filled out a prescription pad note and handed it to my mother. After she left his office, she opened the note. "Don't read or watch the news," it said. The doctor later explained that his patients with higher success rates are the ones who limit the amount of negativity in their lives. For the most part, the news (especially the first page or beginning of the evening news) is negative.

This is why, at talks in the past, I have ripped off the front page of a newspaper and said, "If you must read the news, at least start on page 2."

So, I say to you, if you want to limit the amount of negativity in your life, read and watch as little news as possible. If you decide to watch or read the news regularly, at least balance it with more positive things during the rest of your day.

Now, let's discuss the types of impact you can have. I'd like to give you some strategies for having your desired level of impact and influence.

Professional ImpACT

Impact Your Business/Personal Brand/the World

If you are running a business and want to grow that business while making it impact the world, in my experience, you have to do at least these two things well:

1. Clearly define your why and make sure all of your actions are aligned with that why. Since we discussed this earlier, you already have the format for achieving this. If you haven't done this yet, this is another push to do so. In interview after interview, my guests can tell me in detail what their why truly is. This isn't a coincidence.
2. Be a problem-solver. T. Harv Eker, who wrote *Secrets of the Millionaire Mind*, shared this during our time together: "You need to be a problem-solver, not an opportunity-seeker." The people who are really thriving and really crushing it with their business and their impact are those who are solving problems and not just looking for more opportunities.

So, here is a question for you to answer: what problem are you solving?

When I asked myself this question years ago, here is what I came up with: As an interviewer of the world's top entrepreneurs and thought leaders, the problem I'm solving is that people now have access to too much information (including much misinformation), yet people are still struggling with what actions to take. I feel this is because so much conflicting information has led to inaction for a lot of people. I help them learn what top leaders are all doing so that they know which action has the best chance of yielding the right results. In short, I help them avoid the manholes that many others have already fallen down so that they can avoid these manholes and achieve more efficiently than those trying to sift through misinformation.

Deliver Massive Value

In Gary Vaynerchuk's great book *Jab, Jab, Jab, Right Hook*, he notes that you should be giving and giving and giving before you ever ask for something. Whether that means you bring value to the relationship multiple times before you ever try to cash in or whether that relates to giving on social media over and over before ever asking the audience to buy from you, the message is this: make sure your clients see you as such a value deliverer that they can't imagine not having you as a partner. You can do this by giving to them before they expect it.

How can you deliver massive value? If you want to have an impact and grow your business, you need to define your why, figure out what problem you can solve, and find those who need that problem solved. You then have to deliver massive value.

Here is the great news: if you have the right why in place, if you are solving a problem that helps others in a positive and inspiring way, and if you are delivering the right kind of value, you can't help but have a positive impact on the world in the process.

Personal ImpACT

Impact on Your Personal Life/the Lives of Others/Your Legacy

More great news. Even if you're not an entrepreneur, if you decide on a purpose statement that has a positive impact on others and you live by that statement, help other people with their problems, and try to give more than you take or receive, you'll also impact the world.

As mentioned earlier, your impact doesn't have to be grandiose. Every day, people have a positive impact by paying for someone's coffee; holding the door for someone; or by helping someone shovel their driveway, push their car in the snow, walk across the street, or carry their groceries.

Even just smiling rather than frowning can have a positive impact on others. During our interviews, social media influencers, such as Bruce Van Horn and Gary Loper, shared how someone following them on social media has reached out to note that a Tweet at the right time actually saved their life. In other words, that person may have been going down a deep spiral, but the right words at the right time gave them a new perspective. I was watching the Netflix series *Chasing Cameron* the other day, and the kids in the show, who have millions of followers, noted they had received similar comments.

I haven't had someone reach out to say that one of my posts saved their life, but I have had many say that my posts have inspired them into an action that changed their life or put a smile on their face when they needed it most.

Just sharing positive social media posts could be the way you deliver massive value. Your why could be simply to bring a smile to someone's face when they need it most, and that could also be the problem you're solving.

Are you starting to believe that it could be you who has the kind of impact the world needs right now? I hope I have shown you that anyone, anywhere can have an impact. It all starts with simply deciding to take action.

Now, there's just one question left: are you ready for ACTion?

Act 2

THRIVING

Success Key 1
PRACTICE THE LAW OF ACTION

D id you buy *The Secret* DVD or book? Did you practice the Law of Attraction? Did it, on its own, change your life? I'm thinking if it did, you wouldn't be seeking new answers in relation to achieving success. After all, *The Secret* implied that practicing the Law of Attraction was the only thing you ever had to do to achieve lifelong success.

Ever wonder why (besides Oprah's stamp of approval, of course) millions initially bought that DVD and book each month and why millions of people didn't immediately change their lives, despite so many of them being so optimistic that change would occur in short order?

First of all, let me say that I do believe, as *The Secret* revealed, we draw positive energy and things to our lives if we are positive and vice versa. I like some of the ideas in the book, respect the people (Jack Canfield, Lisa Nichols, Bob Proctor, John Assaraf) featured on *The Secret* DVD, and feel sure that the advice drew many new people to the personal and professional development field.

So, what I'm about to say is certainly not my way of attacking the book, DVD, or the content itself. But, in my opinion, the global discovery of the Law of Attraction alone didn't change millions of lives. Perhaps a few thousand were changed in terms of long-term impact. The same will most likely happen if you read this book but don't apply, create, and cement the habits discussed here.

What I want to address, however, is an important law that was missing from *The Secret*, a law that works in tandem with the Law of Attraction—a law that some say everyone realized had to be applied *with* the Law of Attraction after watching or reading *The Secret*.

After interviewing so many enlightened super-achievers (including some featured in *The Secret* itself), I can tell you the one law that is absolutely crucial to ensuring the Law of Attraction has the impact you desire. Are you ready for it? I'm referring to . . .

The Law of ACTion

Let me give you an example of how the Law of Action and Attraction can be used together to help you crush your goals, assuming you are also using the other strategies presented in this book.

To be fair, the Law of Attraction can work in helping you achieve your goals every now and then (even by coincidence, in some cases) because the vibration side of the Law of Attraction *has truly always worked.* But the odds of it working to its full capacity without you taking action is very slim.

As I've heard many a wise leader say, "Hope is not a business strategy."

So, here is an example. Late in January 2013, I decided on my goals for the year. I never set my goals on January first, as that is a recipe for failure as the statistics well demonstrate. In fact, according to *Forbes* magazine and Brain Stats, just 8 percent of people achieve their New Year's resolutions/goals.

One of the goals I set was to share the bill as a speaker with an international speaker I hadn't yet shared the bill with. So, I wrote out a list of possible speakers. On the top of the list, I put Deepak Chopra's name.

Based on the Law of Attraction lessons alone, I would simply have to put my intention out there, visualize it, put it on my vision board, send out the right vibrations, and perhaps wait for my call.

I can tell you, with almost absolute certainty, that had I chosen that route, my goal would not have been achieved that year because Deepak rarely does talks on cards with other speakers. In fact, he only had one such talk booked in that capacity that entire year, and the event organizers were basically done looking for additional speakers at that point.

A couple of weeks passed after I put Deepak on my list, and I realized I hadn't taken action on my goal of sharing the bill with an internationally known speaker. Within a day of this realization, I determined the steps I would need to take to achieve this goal.

The first was to look online to see where the speakers I was hoping to share the bill with were speaking and then explore a possible fit. I decided to check Deepak's upcoming schedule since he was first on my list. It turned out he was speaking at just one conference that I could locate: the Emergent Learning Conference. I reached out to the Emergent Learning Conference the following Monday morning (a day before the opportunity to be involved closed completely), and within a week, I was added to the bill. Thanks to the Law of Action *combined with* the Law of Attraction, I achieved my goal.

Here's the interesting part. When I spoke to the organizer of the conference, Anne Berube, I could tell she had never heard of me, and at this stage, the conference organizers weren't actively reaching out for other speakers. If I had used the Law of Attraction on its own, what would my odds have been of achieving this goal so quickly, especially when the organizers hadn't heard of me and were near the closing of their bookings? Fairly low, I'm certain.

Now, here's the best part. If you have already practiced the Law of Attraction (or even if you haven't), what I'm suggesting you do is incorporate the following formula into your Law of Attraction work, rather than going against what you've already been doing. The formula, which I have labelled the Law of Action Formula, is, as follows:

$$G \div T + A + A = S$$

**Goals ÷ Time (i.e., breaking your goals into pieces) +
Action + Attraction = Success**

To illustrate, here is an excerpt from an earlier books in which I share an example from leadership guru Robin Sharma (author of *The Monk Who Sold His*

Ferrari and ten more international bestselling books) practicing this formula in his life and career:

Deciding a life change was in order, Robin started writing what would become the international bestselling book *The Monk Who Sold His Ferrari.*

What a lot of people don't know or realize about the early days of the book is that at this point in time, it was far from on its way to becoming a bestseller.

Starting with just 500 copies of the (self-published) book sitting in his parents' living room, Robin was selling copies of the books just one at a time from the back from his father's car, supplementing book sales with client speaking engagements.

Then something amazing happened. During a book signing in a Toronto Chapters store, following the consignment of *The Monk Who Sold His Ferrari* book, Robin just happened to meet Ed Carson, president and CEO of HarperCollins Canada.

The two had a conversation during which Robin explained his philosophies about leadership and life, and shortly thereafter, Robin and his Monk book were signed to Harper Collins.

It's almost the makings of a made-for-TV movie of the week, but perhaps it was the Law of Attraction at work as Robin was surely focused on achieving the goal of bringing his inspirational book to the masses.

Over one million copies later, it's safe to say that Robin Sharma has arrived.

As a side note, *The Monk Who Sold His Ferrari* has now sold over five million copies. But the question is once again posed: if Robin hadn't practiced the Law of Action (putting the self-published version together, selling the books out of the back of his father's car, and, most importantly, approaching the book store about doing a book signing and staying for the signing, even though few people were approaching him), do you think the book would be at one million in sales, let alone five million? It's safe to say the answer is at least "it's unlikely."

Yes, the Law of Attraction was at work, but it was practiced equally with the Law of Action. Robin's goals could have been to become an international bestselling author or thought leader. The mini-goals were the steps he took (self-publishing); the actions were attending the book-signing and selling from the back of his car; the attraction was probably the attitude with which he proceeded in forward motion; and, of course, the outcome equals success, significance, and enlightenment.

I can give you hundreds of examples that prove this formula and prove that the Law of Action is as necessary, perhaps more necessary, than the Law of Attraction. On the other hand, I cannot give you hundreds of examples of how the reverse is true.

As such, Success Key 1 is, if you want to crush your goals and achieve real and lifelong success, you need to practice the Law of Action formula: $G \div T + A + A = S$.

Questions to Ask/Steps to Take
- What three goals do you want to crush?
- What mini-steps can you take right now?
- What reward will you give yourself for taking these steps?
- When will you begin, and how will you make sure you start and continue?
- What deadline will you set for achieving these goals?

Success Key 2
EXPAND YOUR COMFORT ZONE

I n 2002, I moved across the country and accepted a position with a Global 1000 organization. At the same time, I tried my hand at putting a stage play into a fringe festival.

Submitting the play wasn't really outside my comfort zone as I was directing and not a central actor. However, acting in front of an audience was certainly outside my comfort zone at the time. At the end of the show's run, I was driving across town with one of the show's actors when he said, "Hey, man, I heard about this stand-up comedy workshop taking place at the university. I'm going to attend. Interested?"

"That sounds terrifying," I said.

Public speaking is the number one fear in the world, ranking even higher than death.

So, yes, in response to the stand-up comedy workshop, I said, "That sounds terrifying. I'm in!" I mean, if you're going to conquer a fear, you have to face it head on.

I jumped into the workshop, and at the three-week mark, I found myself at a comedy club (well, a dive of a nightclub acting as a comedy club that evening) and discovered five minutes before show time that I was expected to do a set of comedy that night.

I started sweating profusely, went into the bathroom to look for an exit window, and then thought seriously about darting out the front door of the club. Thankfully, I didn't. That night—and the seven hundred shows that followed—helped me discover my passion as a speaker and gave me the tools to tackle a career in speaking.

Was I good that night? Absolutely not! I was horrible. I told my first joke without the mic turned on. I didn't remember how to adjust the mic stand, and I was so nervous that I bombed. I bombed night after night for the first couple of hundred shows—at least.

At the same time, I learned one of the most important success keys I have ever discovered: you cannot achieve at your highest level (or become a super-achiever) without determining your comfort zone and repeatedly expanding it. This truth has been echoed in conversation after conversation with the world's highest achievers.

For instance, Chalene Johnson (creator of the highly popular Turbo Jam fitness program, *New York Times* bestselling author, and top-rated podcaster) shared with us that when she told her father about the success she was having with the Turbo Jam program at a local gym, he said, "Great, now how are you going to share it with the world?" She hadn't even seen that as an option. It was certainly outside her comfort zone.

When we interviewed Grammy nominee Alan Frew (lead singer of the popular Canadian band Glass Tiger), he shared that he was so nervous during early gigs he used to vomit behind the amps between songs. In fact, he was so nervous during one performance that he actually ran away from the club, and the band had to chase him down.

Both Chalene and Alan had to take these steps outside their comfort zones to become the people they are today. Chalene's Turbo Jam program has resulted in six million DVDs sold, and Alan's performances have been seen by millions—something not every Canadian artist can say.

The best part is this: if you haven't discovered your passion yet, stepping outside your comfort zone regularly is often the quickest path to discovering it.

This alone can transform your life and career. If you're a member of our newsletter group, I'll be sending a video out covering the power of passion. If you're not a member, you can join by visiting www.thatspeakerguy.com

Passion is the most common trait of the highest achievers we have interviewed. All have found their passion and are living on purpose. Our video will include a form designed to help you discover your passion and/or to direct, define, and fuel it.

I don't claim in a short guide like this to be able to help you conquer a fear like public speaking or jumping out of a plane, but I will claim that comfort zone expansion is necessary for you to become the you that you were meant to be.

Oh, and if you want more insight into this success key, you can check out TEDx Talk, How People Crush Fears and Expand Comfort Zones which you can find at www. coreypoirier.ca. As noted in the video, if your comfort zone is small, you can expand it by starting small and taking very tiny steps outside it. It could be as simple as reading a book or talking to someone on Skype, if that is currently outside your natural comfort zone.

If you didn't check out the Comfort Zone expansion video, How People Crush Fears and Expand Comfort Zones, on the website above, here is an exercise I'd love to see you try.

First, I suggest you draw a circle like the one below where I listed my early comfort zone items and those initially outside of my comfort zone. Then, list some of the things that are inside your current comfort zone and things that you would like to do or achieve that are outside of your zone. Make sure to list the small ones that fall just outside your comfort zone first as those are the ones you'll tackle first.

There are no right or wrong answers, but now that you have put your comfort zone circle to paper, here are the steps I suggest you take to start the process of expanding your comfort zone and using the visual to achieve your biggest goals:

- Step 1: Set your goals.
- Step 2: Determine which goals are closest to your comfort zone and which ones are furthest outside.
- Step 3: List the steps required to achieve each goal.

- Step 4: Start taking mini-steps outside your natural comfort zone, reward yourself for each mini-step taken, and watch your comfort zone expand ever so slightly.

Note: Determine the rewards before you begin taking steps.

The following quotation by Neale Donald Walsch summarizes this principle nicely: "Life begins at the end of your comfort zone."

Questions to Ask/Steps to Take

- In what ways do you want to step outside your comfort zone? (Make sure to write them out.)
- What smaller steps are needed to reach a larger step? (Make sure to write these down as well.)
- When will you start and when will you reach your goal? (As Stephen Covey says in his classic *The 7 Habits of Highly Effective People*, "Begin with the end in mind.")
- What steps can you take starting now?
- How will you reward those steps?

Summary

Determine your comfort zone and find small ways to expand it daily.

During our interview with Rain Pryor (daughter of iconic comedian Richard Pryor), she shared that her grandfather told her to do every job she had in her life like she was working at her absolute passion. This is similar to my grandfather's advice of giving 100 percent to every job I do, even if it isn't my first choice. This is great advice based on everything I have learned since.

Before we get to Success Key 3, which also relates to our biggest challenge, let's talk for a second about how we can use the first two keys to crush our goals regularly. To use the first two keys (taking action and stepping outside your comfort zone) to crush your goals, you need to do the following:

- Step 1: Determine and write down your goals.
- Step 2: Map out how you will take action (breaking the actions required to achieve your goals into smaller pieces so you can take action on each small piece daily).
- Step 3: Determine and list which goals are inside your comfort zone and which ones are outside.
- Step 4: Start taking daily, small steps to tackle the goals just outside your comfort zone first, so you get used to accomplishing goals. Then, tackle the ones on the edge of your comfort zone until you are ready to tackle the ones further outside your comfort zone. Track your progress.
- Step 5: Give yourself a reward each time you accomplish a goal to motivate further action. What rewards will you give yourself each time?
- Step 6: Reflect.

Success Key 3

LEARN THE POWER OF
FOCUS AND BEING ALL IN

This key was discovered by accident, during interviews with many of the world's busiest and most enlightened super-achievers.

Case in point: Jack Canfield is busy doing talks across the globe, running multiple businesses, releasing books and audio products regularly, and growing the highly successful *Chicken Soup for the Soul* series. Arlene Dickinson (*Dragons' Den*) is busy appearing on a hit show, presenting at many engagements, raising four daughters, releasing books, operating Canada's largest female-owned marketing company, and speaking to the media regularly. Tony Horton is busy operating the P90x empire and multiple related projects.

Yet, Jack, Arlene, and Tony (and thousands just like them) were able to give me their full attention during interviews, not once distracted by phones or incoming email. As I learned during our interview, Dr. David Suzuki doesn't even own a cellphone.

At the same time, many people can't imagine spending minutes without the aid of their iPhone or Android, and people daily are walking into items because they can't look up from their phone long enough to see what is happening around them.

When we had speaker Mike Lipkin on the show, he described this ability to single-task (not trying to juggle a device and a person) as being "all in" with whatever we are doing at the time.

I think this demonstrates a great point. Jack, Arlene, Tony, Mike—and if I can add myself—we all have smart phones and access to similar technology. It's not that we don't make use of this technology; it's just that when we are with people, we are all in with them, and when we are with our devices, we are all in with our devices.

I'm including myself here as if I knew the importance of going all in naturally and did it already. I didn't! I was a mess when I purchased my first BlackBerry, checking my phone like crazy and replying to every single call, text, or email the second they came in. It took me a while to take the power back.

The difference is that we (and I'm taking liberty in including myself) simply took action in finding a way to remove distraction so we can be all in when we need to be, whether with a person or a device.

Let me share a short excerpt from my fictional *Standing Ovations* book that illustrates why I feel this is important enough to be its own principle:

> ***Can you imagine paying the equivalent of $100 for a ticket to see the Beatles back in the 1960s and then seeing one of them answer his phone to text someone half-way through a song? For John to take a call from Yoko, perhaps? There would have been a riot, or at least a lot of unhappy (and vocal) fans. So why is it more acceptable now?***

Most people tell their clients, associates, family, and friends that they have to leave their phones on "just in case." If you can separate yourself by being the one who is all in, doing whatever is most important to you and your career and not trying to multitask and juggle many things at once, you'll have a distinct advantage. It's kind of ironic that practicing good etiquette is now a business strategy.

Another reason that focus is so significant is because we, as humans, are not designed for multitasking. We need to get back to what I call single-tasking. I think it's time we begin making single-tasking the new sexy.

Various studies estimate it takes people minutes to gain focus again after becoming distracted for mere seconds. This strategy of being all in puts you in a better position than those being distracted all day.

Also, even though it sounds simple, most people have a very difficult time forwarding their phone, turning it on silent, not looking at it, and so on. If you make the effort and succeed, you will be doing what most cannot—and this almost always works in your favor.

I was recently interviewing a doctor on our show who shared that checking phones regularly has become such an ingrained habit because the act itself (of hearing an email message and checking it) releases dopamine and endorphins. So, it's no longer just a habit; it's an addiction. But I believe in you—and I believe that you can break this habit (or addiction).

Finally, the simple practice of saying *no* to your phone or device, or whatever the distraction, opens you up for applying the most powerful productivity tool I know.

How do you practice this key? By removing the distraction in the first place (i.e., turning off your device when you're in front of someone else, not accepting certain tasks or meetings, and saying no to those devices or tasks).

I used to think that high achievers were so productive because they knew what to say *yes* to. A quotation by Sir Richard Branson emphasizes this point: "Say yes to everything and figure out how to do it later."

After thousands of interviews, I learned the highest of enlightened super-achievers know what to say no to so they can say yes to something else. I actually think Richard Branson means we should say yes to the things we want to do and figure out how to do them later, but until I sit with him and ask, it's all speculation. (Edit: I've since been led to believe that his quote was slightly different. My understanding now is that he said, "Say yes to the things you love and figure out how to do it later.")

The difference between saying yes and no sounds small, but it is massive. Consider the example of comedian Gerry Dee (star of the hit show *Mr. D*), a super-achiever who appeared on our show. During his visit, he shared that he took a gig on Halloween when his daughter was two years old and missed taking her out trick-or-treating. After the gig, he realized it wasn't worth it to miss out on such an occasion, and he decided, going forward, that he would say no to any gig that interfered with an important family event.

Let's provide an example of how you can use this knowledge to get more done and how saying no can be a powerful productivity strategy.

We will start by looking at a task list. If you don't write down your goals, the odds of achieving them is small. Not only that, but your odds of earning increased income also goes up dramatically if you have written goals. That's already such an advantage that making the habit of starting to write things down could be a game changer for you on its own. In fact, I was just reading a Harvard MBA study on this exact subject.

But, let's assume you write out your goals and a task list. How can you use the power of no versus yes when you write down your daily tasks and when you consider the tasks that enter your life unexpectedly each day?

Let's say you wrote the following task list last night, even predicting some of the normal unforeseen variables that come into your day:

- Read a chapter in a personal development book
- Write post for new blog
- Spend time on Facebook
- Return calls hourly
- Reply to emails hourly
- Drive between client offices
- Visit family members
- Attend to interruptions from coworkers
- Take part in various meetings

The goal is to remain proactive rather than reactive. Normally, a high-achiever or a producer would have such a list, and he/she would essentially say yes to everything, but prioritize between the tasks using an A, B, C system or a 1, 2, 3 system. Simply completing these steps would put that person (or you) ahead of more than 90 percent of the people in almost any profession.

In contrast, enlightened super-achievers would say no to certain tasks so they could then prioritize the rest. As an example, if we look at the task list here, enlightened super-achievers would find ways to avoid the distractions from coworkers (which may mean not coming into the office at peak disruption times if that's possible or turning their phones on silent while they are with customers so they are not taking calls), reduce the number or length of meetings (especially the non-essential ones), turn unproductive driving time into a learning experience by listening to CDs, check and reply to email and phone calls just twice a day, shift family meetings from weekdays to the weekend (when there is more time), and reduce or eliminate the amount of time spent on social media.

This level of focus will certainly impact a person's productivity and allow him/her to say yes to other, perhaps more productive, tasks during the day.

Based on years of research, I would say that the way we manage our day has more impact on our ability to achieve our biggest goals than any other action. We all have twenty-four hours in a day, yet some manage five to six times more than others in those same hours. I am convinced it's because they know how to remain proactive and when to say no.

As a final note on this success key, if you want a strategy to help you determine what to say yes and no to, here's what I do. As I noted in Act 1, I developed a short mission statement years ago. My mission statement is that every day I strive to entertain, motivate, inspire, donate, and educate.

When I get asked to take on something new, I ask myself whether it will align with at least one of the elements in my mission statement and, therefore, my larger purpose. If the answer is no, then it's an easy no for me. If the answer is yes to one to three of those elements, I consider the opportunity. If it aligns with four or five of the elements of my mission statement, it's an easy yes. My decision-making process is really that simple. It leaves me with little regret and allows me to be completely confident in my decision.

Questions to Ask/Steps to Take

- What tasks are you currently saying yes to that you should be saying no to?
- How will you determine what tasks you will say no to?
- How will you say no?
- What will you use the new time for?

Summary

Have you written down your core purpose or focus so that you know which tasks support it and which take away from it?

Start taking a proactive mindset, turning your phone to silent and/or forwarding your calls, determining what your focus areas should be, identifying your goals and the steps required to meet/achieve them, tracking your time for a week to determine what interferes with your current path to achieving your goals, making your daily task list, tracking when something is about to interfere, and saying no as often as possible when the task at hand will distract you from your core focus.

Now that we've covered the first three keys, I want to share what I feel is your greatest challenge in today's digital world and also one of the greatest solutions. This challenge and the solution will bring us to Success Key 4 and Success Key 5.

Your Challenge

The most common complaint I hear from friends and clients these days is, "I can't keep up with everything."

I've heard the estimate that all of the information in the world doubles every twelve months. If you can't keep up now, what's going to happen in a year or five years' time?

Magazines hit us with conflicting information. Facebook, LinkedIn, and Twitter provide unlimited news feeds. Google provides access to an answer (both factual and inaccurate) for every question. YouTube videos, voice mails, texts, and emails inundate us on a daily basis. As a result, we have entered what I like to call the information heavy, knowledge/wisdom light generation.

They say knowledge is power. I once had a client who clarified this saying by arguing, "*Applied* knowledge is power." I had to agree with his revision: having knowledge and not applying it is like having an idea and not doing anything with it or having deodorant and not using it.

The problem now is, with the amount of information coming at us, how can we efficiently sort through the information to get the knowledge we seek?

Success Key 4 and 5

REMEMBER THAT APPLIED KNOWLEDGE IS POWER AND CHOOSE YOUR LEARNING SOURCES WISELY

Those who can sort through information to obtain knowledge and wisdom more quickly and then apply that knowledge will inherit the future—or at least become a leader within it.

In fact, there is an endless supply of guides, reports, and books (just like this one you are reading) that you must sift through to find the knowledge that will make the difference. My goal is to make sure this book gives you the knowledge and wisdom—not just information—you need to thrive.

The Solution

Here's the great thing about the challenge of having access to so much (often contradicting) information. The same sources that provide us with access to information also allow us to personalize what we receive. For the first time in history, we have the opportunity to learn on demand.

In the past, your learning options were essentially grab a book and start reading, listen to your daily news program, read your local paper, or register for a course taught by an instructor in a classroom.

Today, you can choose the podcast you want to hear, select from a barrage of news programs, read niche publications, follow your favorite influencers online, subscribe to online membership sites, and learn for free from sources like TED. com, *Success* magazine, and even YouTube.

In fact, when people ask me how I took my own presentations from what they were years ago to what they are today, I tell them they can find the answer by visiting YouTube and typing in the words "Steve Job's presentations."

The challenge remains, however, to choose sources wisely—unless you want to be flooded with "information" and then separate what is credible from what isn't. As an example, we spend thousands of hours seeking out the best of the best for our *Conversations With PASSION!* radio show, and then we drill further to pick the best portions from the interviews to broadcast.

By subscribing to our radio show, for example, you can gain insight from trusted sources, like Mari Smith and Pat Flynn—rather than trying to gain this same insight reading article after article or even trying to figure out who the best of the best are in the first place. Having such a source like our show shortens the amount of time you spend gaining insight since we have already done the work for you.

In spending two hours a month listening to the new episodes of our show, you can gain knowledge that might take twenty hours of searching online if you had to go article by article. Magazines like *Success* or an Inner Circle membership like the one offered by Jack Canfield also help you boost productivity by providing with excellent knowledge in a concise way.

As an example, I have recently subscribed to John Lee Dumas' membership website, *Podcaster's Paradise,* to learn how he successfully and quickly launched his popular *Entrepreneur on Fire* podcast. (The podcast began averaging over five hundred thousand listens a month in less than two years.) For less than one hundred dollars a month as a member, I'm skipping past mistakes that I'm confident would surely cost me thousands of dollars and perhaps hundreds of hours to learn in the trenches.

How did I discover John? Well, we had him on our show, and I have been on his. John was doing the work to find the best guests for his shows, and I was drawn to his show since it saved me time trying to discover influencers with online searches and other methods.

What was the result of me joining and becoming active in the *Podcaster's Paradise* membership site and learning what mistakes to avoid? When we launched our radio show on iTunes (two years after the initial launch of our broadcast), the show reached the top two in marketing and top six in business multiple times during the first month of the launch. Keep in mind, we had to compete with more than 375,000 other podcasts to get these results. Not bad for a one hundred dollar monthly investment. Oh, and because I joined *Podcaster's Paradise* early, I simply had to invest that one hundred dollars per month for four months to receive lifetime access.

Why would you want to spend hours trying to find similar knowledge and insight when you can pick trusted sources and subscribe to their information so that it comes directly to you? This way, you don't have to search for or sort through the bounty of *unhelpful* information that exists.

A similar example of using the power of tapping your trusted sources came when we asked the great Zig Ziglar, who was in the later stage of his life, and Susan Manion MacDonald, who was battling terminal cancer and had two months to live, how they chose what to read.

I chose Zig and Susan as they both were facing a shortened amount of learning time. I was intrigued by the idea of what one might choose to learn if he or she knew learning time was limited. Ziglar told us he only read things that were true and/or would improve his life. He wanted to grow every single day, regardless of how few days he had left.

In Susan's case, she wanted to learn how she might defeat her disease. She put cancer in remission as a result of the knowledge she gained through what she read in just two months because she used that two months to learn how she could turn her body into an alkaline state in which many say cancer can't survive. She gave us one of the best strategies to determine how to gain the best knowledge and decide what books to read. In Susan's case, she approached the people she admired and trusted and asked them what they were reading in relation to optimal health. Anything that was suggested multiple times was what she tackled first. The more times a resource was recommended, the more quickly she sought to read it. Smartphones and Netflix are other great examples of ways to obtain content on demand, and both can be your best friend—if you use them correctly—because both give you immediate access to information that can take your life to the next level, whether it be a TED Talk, documentary, video, or online resource.

Summary

So, what is the take-away message? Instead of being inundated by the sheer amount of available information, clearly determine your go-to sources.

In the past, these go-to sources may have been limited to your local news channel or daily newspaper. Today, these sources could include podcasts, books, digital or hard copy material, radio shows, niche publications, social media accounts or online sites of influencers, membership groups, and so on.

Where do you start? You need to find a strategy to find the best of the best: what podcasts to listen to, which influencers to follow, and what books to read—to name just a few examples. As Susan demonstrated, try approaching people you admire or people who have achieved what you want to achieve and ask them what they are reading or what books they see as game changers.

Bonus Success Key

(KEY 6)
PRACTICE DOES MAKE PERFECT

'm a big believer that whenever possible, you should try to over- deliver. So, I decided to include a sixth (and highly powerful) success key. To demonstrate this key, let me share that we interviewed *Success* magazine publisher Darren Hardy when he was just releasing his brilliant book *The Compound Effect*.

The premise of this book is simple and powerful: if you want to achieve at the highest level of success, the surest path is to decide what you want to achieve, determine the steps you need to take to get there, and practice the steps (take action) over and over again. Each time you practice, your results will compound.

As mentioned in Act 1, Malcolm Gladwell, in *Outliers*, talks about the ten-thousand-hour rule; he argues it takes ten thousand hours to master anything you set your mind to. In my experience, this is a fact.

I call this rule the non-talent factor because it allows us, regardless of natural talent, to eventually become a master at that which we are passionate about. I had a great conversation with world-renowned fiddler Natalie MacMaster about this exact subject. I also spoke in-depth with Allan Andrews, the founder of a hockey school that has allowed him to work with the likes of Sidney Crosby, Brad

Richards, and Brad Marchand. Interestingly, both conversations came around to the subject of hockey. Here's what each had to say.

Natalie MacMaster's Take

Natalie shared with me, "Funny enough, I've seen people achieve extraordinary things with ordinary talent throughout my career, and I've discovered that energy, passion, and attitude play a big part in a person's success—career or otherwise. I feel blessed to have been given such a gift, but I don't know that I would have honed it and turned it into a career without the knowledge that you have to use it so that you won't lose it."

I asked, "Do you feel we can sometimes overstate the talent factor?" Natalie's answer: "For sure. Don't get me wrong; it plays a major part, but you can have a great talent, and if you never do the work, you may never fully realize it. I mean, Wayne Gretzky was born with an obvious talent, but he also did the work. That is the way with everything in life. If you want to be good, you have to practice, you have to hone it. You also have to take action and make your own opportunities. Talent alone won't take you very far."

Allan Andrews' Take

"Some of the most successful guys have natural talent," Allan told me. "But it's what they did with that talent that matters. I've seen players who didn't have that level of talent go on to have extraordinary NHL careers because of the amount of time they practiced. A book called *Talent Is Overrated, by Geoffrey Colvin,* says, 'If you deliberately practice in the right way, you'll go much further than someone who doesn't.' I think that speaks volumes about the fact that talent isn't the only factor in a person's success—in any field, in fact."

Looking at Natalie and Allan's quotes, I have to add that, for my own part, people say to me often, "Wow, you seem so multitalented, given all that you do." But, if these people were looking at that twenty-year-old who hadn't read a book, barely graduated high school, failed remedial typing in business school, and was virtually tone deaf when he started playing guitar, they surely wouldn't feel that way.

What's the difference between that twenty-year-old and the forty-two-year-old writing this today? The difference is practice. *In the time between* twenty and forty, I practiced, practiced, and practiced some more. Each time, I got better at something, I was able to use the learned knowledge to tackle the next thing more quickly and easily, and once I discovered that if I practiced enough, I could learn to do almost anything, my newfound confidence made tackling the next thing much simpler.

Then, sure enough, my momentum started to build. Before I knew it, I was crushing goals monthly—goals that would have taken me years to reach before.

So, Success Key 6 is the dedication to practice hour upon hour and to take the new knowledge you gain through your practice and compound it with the knowledge you have from the past so that your knowledge and skill grow exponentially.

Now that we have discussed six of the keys that can transform your life, why don't we summarize how they work together to bring about major transformation?

Success Key 1: PrACTice the Law of ACTion
Decide what you want to draw to your life and achieve in your life, but rather than simply practicing the Law of Attraction, add in the Law of Action and practice both together.

Success Key 2: Expand Your Comfort Zone
Determine what's inside and outside your comfort zone and start taking baby steps outside of your comfort zone. As your comfort zone expands, start taking larger steps.

Success Key 3: Learn the Power of Focus and Being All In
Practice being "all in" in everything you do, even when this means turning off, forwarding, or silencing your smartphone and email notifications. Focus on the task at hand, and start saying no when necessary so you can say yes to the things that matter.

Success Key 4: Remember That Applied Knowledge Is Power

Find an efficient way to get to the important knowledge that will transform your life so that you can apply that knowledge sooner.

Success Key 5: Choose Your Learning Sources Wisely

Choose your sources, determine how they gain their knowledge, and proceed accordingly. In a time when learning on demand is possible, choose your sources wisely so you can make the most effective use of time. If someone else is spending thousands of hours seeking out the information you're looking for, perhaps you can access it from them in a more efficient manner. This could mean subscribing to their social media pages, podcasts, or radio shows; reading their writing; asking what they are reading; joining their membership circles; or taking them out for lunch and picking their brain.

Success Key 6: PrACTice Does Make Perfect

Remain steady and practice, practice, practice. You will master what it is you want to master if you just practice enough—and in the right way.

Act 3

ENLIGHTENED

Step 1

HAVE YOU BEEN TAKING YOUR VITAMIN P (PASSION)?

I asked Trish Stratus, former female wrestling champion and owner of the largest single-location yoga studio in Canada, what key ingredient made The Rock, Stone Cold Steve Austin, and Hulk Hogan the most successful professional wrestlers. Trish replied, without hesitation, that their passion far exceeded that of others in the industry.

(The late) *Trailer Park Boys* actor John Dunsworth, who plays trailer park supervisor, Mr. Jim Lahey, shared with me a story about how a number of young actors were on the set of the TV show *Haven* at the end of a fourteen-hour day. They were all exhausted, but John, age sixty-five at the time, was dancing around asking what they were going to do next. The young actors asked him how he had so much energy after such a grueling day. John told them he had long ago discovered that acting was his love, and if you do what you love, it's hard to get tired because you're never really working. In other words, he had lots of energy because the day wasn't long to him. It was just another day filled with passion.

I mentioned earlier that Robin Sharma shared his feeling with me that, "Many people die at twenty but don't get buried until eighty—the walking dead,

I call them!" I think the walking dead are the people who haven't yet discovered their passion and, therefore, are not yet working toward their life purpose.

I've heard statistics that suggest only 5 percent of us spend our days pursuing our passion. Whether that number is accurate or not, I certainly would not say anything negative about someone who hasn't yet uncovered their passion. I know many people who are trying to find their passion and simply haven't yet. I know others who simply don't know why it's important to find their passion in the first place—perhaps because they haven't experienced the benefits firsthand.

Still, I personally know how important it is to find that passion because the day I officially started to become enlightened was the day I uncovered my passion. Even though I know the importance of this passion now, I didn't uncover it until I was in my mid-twenties, on the day I *officially retired*.

What do I mean by "officially retired"? Did I move to a beach with a lawn chair in tow and bid farewell to the life I had known? Did I win the lottery or decide that I would never have to earn another penny? Not at all.

But the day I discovered my passion, I ceased "working" and began "living." The fact I was no longer working, or simply doing a job, is what retirement is all about. Sure, I spend time everyday living my purpose, but I tell everyone, "If you catch me 'working,' please let me know, and I'll stop."

Before discovering my passion, I spent many a day soaked in self-pity. I couldn't understand what my purpose was and how I could contribute. I even battled hypochondria and anxiety. My hypochondria disappeared after I started pursuing my passion. I believe that's because it's difficult to be a hypochondriac while living every day with passion. One requires pessimistic thinking, the other optimistic.

So how did I discover my passion and perhaps begin to become more enlightened? Believe it or not, it all started on a stand-up comedy stage.

In 2002, I was directing a stage play at a fringe festival in Atlantic, Canada. At the end of a seven-day run, one of the actors asked me if I wanted to check out a three-week stand-up comedy workshop at a local university. I agreed, albeit reluctantly. Within a week, I was sitting in a class, learning about the history of stand-up comedy and the proper way to adjust a mic stand. After two weeks in class, we learned that for our third week, we would attend a performance to watch comedians at a local bar.

We arrived at the bar that night and discovered five minutes before the show that we were, in fact, the comedians who would entertain. I bolted to the bathroom to look for an exit window. There was no window. When I came back out into the club, only six of the fifteen in the workshop were still there. I was the seventh.

It was a terrifying experience. I told my first joke without the mic turned on, which garnered zero audience response. It didn't get much better, and I found myself absolutely covered in sweat throughout my seven-minute set.

Despite my better judgement, I returned to the stage the next week and then the next and so on. All in all, I ended up performing some seven hundred times over the course of the next nine years.

I also made an interesting discovery: after the first couple of nights, people at work started to comment that I had an extra jump in my step. In fact, my coworkers began to press as to whether or not I had met a new love interest. In many ways, I guess I had met a love interest, but not the kind they were thinking of.

This was my first taste of living with passion. I was spending just five to ten minutes a week on stage, engaging in public speaking, which has been called the number one fear (above death) for the average person, spending hours preparing material, and paying for my own gas to get to the club.

I was involved in what would become just an extension of my real passion, yet it was carrying over every day into my work and changing my outlook on life. *That is the power of passion.* In truth, my life has never been the same. My hypochondria all but disappeared, and my anxiety has been very limited since.

Oh, and here is some great news about passion. You can live your passion part-time while working at a job you may "like" but not "love." Perhaps your passion will eventually provide the income you need to quit the job you "like." I say "like" rather than dislike because I don't feel anyone should stay in a job they dislike. Life is simply too short.

More great news. You're never too old to uncover your passion. Colonel Sanders started Kentucky Fried Chicken (KFC) at age sixty-five when he found out how low his retirement checks would be. George Foreman became the oldest heavyweight boxing champion at forty-nine, and Mark Victor Hansen and Jack Canfield launched the highly successful *Chicken Soup for the Soul* book series when Jack was forty-eight, I believe, and Mark forty-five. You can find your passion at any age.

Why bother striving to find your passion? Well, when you have discovered your passion, you become excited to wake up and start each day; you can battle colds and flus more readily; you smile more; your heart sings; and people can't help but feed off your passion.

You can watch the passion video at www. coreypoirier.ca to learn how to start the journey toward finding your own passion. Now, I'd like to shift my attention to *purpose*.

If finding your passion helps you become more enlightened, then living on purpose increases your level of enlightenment tenfold. So what's the difference between passion and purpose? They both work together very well, and, in fact, I use a formula to describe the result of combining the two:

PASSION + PURPOSE = SIGNIFICANCE
(profits and impact often result automatically)

From my perspective, the difference between the two is that passion is what you're doing (e.g., performing stand-up comedy), and purpose is why you're doing it (e.g., to entertain people and make them forget about their troubles).

I mentioned earlier that stand-up comedy turned out to be just an extension of my true and real passion. It took a couple of years, but I ultimately discovered that my real passion is keynote speaking.

My real purpose is to inspire, motivate, educate, donate, and entertain through my speaking engagements. This is, in fact, my personal mission (aka purpose) statement: to be the guy who inspires, motivates, educates, donates, and entertains.

Using a well-known example, Disney's purpose, as defined by Walt himself, was "to make people, especially children, happy." Perhaps realizing that adults are simply big children, Disney has changed its purpose in the years since. It is now "to make people happy." I believe that because Disney's cast members know their employer's purpose, they can serve in a way that continues to make the parks the "happiest place on earth." This is the power of knowing my purpose. It allows me to serve and make decisions that stay aligned with my purpose, and it does the same for Disney and their employees.

So, let's shift the focus from Disney to you and discuss how you can find and work toward your purpose. First, you have to discover your passion, and we are providing a quick exercise at the end of this section for you to do just that. Of course, you can also check the passion video at www.coreypoirier.ca as reference above.

Once you know what your passion is, then creating your mission statement is a whole lot easier. Why should you have a mission statement? Almost every successful company (even those you have worked for, perhaps) has a clearly defined mission statement, and I would argue it's even more important for each of us to have a personal mission statement. This holds true even more so for those of us who are self-employed.

So, let's begin. This exercise is really simple, albeit profound and very powerful. All you need to do is fill out the following statement:

My name is _____; my passion is _____, and, therefore, my purpose is _____.

To make it easier, I'll give you an example: my name is Corey Poirier; my passion is speaking to audiences about passion, purpose, legacy, and customer service, and, therefore, my purpose is to inspire, motivate, donate, entertain, and educate.

If you can figure out and fill out this passion + personal mission statement accurately, profits, productivity, fulfillment, and other benefits will soon follow.

Step 2
SELF-CARE

No answer eludes us if we turn to the source of all answers—the stillness within.

—Anonymous

Gandhi and Mother Teresa seemed to embody love. Martin Luther King Jr. was able to love others who would choose to take his life. We spent some time in Memphis this year at the Martin Luther King memorial site, and the more I learned about King, the more in awe I became of his ability to truly love while trying to right wrongs that could frustrate even the most peace-loving person.

The power of acting, working, and serving with love may be one of the most difficult acts one will attempt, and at the same time, it may be one of the most powerful.

When I asked psychologist Ken Pierce his belief about the meaning of life, he said simply, "The meaning of life is love."

If love is this powerful, I knew I had to test the waters in showing love to others, especially if I intended to care for and love myself. So, I set out to (at least once a day) send a text or email or place a call to someone to simply tell them how much they meant to me or how much I appreciated them. By doing so, I aimed to grow my ability to love and be loved.

The result has been astounding in terms of the strength of my relationships with those I have reached out to. Although I can't speak fully to how they feel about it or what your experience will be like, I would love to see you give it a try.

Perhaps right now, while you're reading this, you can take a break and send a text or email or place a call to someone in your life (a business partner, a customer, a supplier, a spouse or girlfriend/boyfriend, a family member, or a friend) and simply tell them why they matter to you or why you appreciate them. I believe firmly that the more you exhibit love to others, the more love you will receive *and* the more you will begin to love yourself.

A number of years ago, after I experienced a trifecta of deaths in my circle of family and friends, I started telling my mother I loved her during each call, text, or email. It has strengthened our relationship in ways I cannot explain, and now I will never have regrets that I didn't share with her how I felt. It has certainly allowed each of us to feel more appreciated by the other.

The invisible impact and ripple effect of spreading this kind of love will certainly do the world little harm and cannot help but do it some good. When we begin to truly receive love, we start to learn how healthy it is to receive. At the same time, when we give the love back, we also begin to discover it's just as healthy to give. This point is important because many people have just as much difficulty receiving love as they do giving it away.

It's also important to note that we should be giving without expecting to receive and vice versa. In this way, we can experience what it means to be altruistic. Learning to give without expectations will improve our well-being and energy and ultimately allow us to better care for ourselves in a way that few do.

Meditation

How comforting to know that all answers are as close as our quiet moments and that each day is a new beginning.
—Anonymous

When I interviewed meditation guru davidji, he shared with me his journey to find a guru who could help him achieve the level of enlightenment he sought. He had become disenchanted with a successful corporate career. Looking for a different path, he heard about a yoga program at the Chopra Wellness Center and signed up.

During his time in the yoga program, he was striving to become more enlightened, and it ended up being Deepak Chopra himself who suggested perhaps davidji should head to India to see if he could find what he was looking for. Indeed, davidji did head to India, and what he found was that the guru was actually inside himself.

This is also how he found his way back to the Chopra Wellness Center where he eventually spent a significant amount of time as the first dean of wellness with the Chopra Wellness Center. Ultimately, davidji found this powerful discovery—that our own guru is within—through meditation. This is the power of meditation.

The sad truth is, although many who read this book will have meditated or may meditate regularly, the vast majority have either tried meditation a few times and given up or have never tried to meditate at all. Many of those same people perhaps think of meditation as some mystical activity that involves believing in things their life experience simply hasn't yet let them believe. Others might envision a skinny yogi dude sitting cross legged.

I do love what davidji says about the fact that it doesn't matter what type of meditation style (guided meditation, stillness, etc.) you practice, as long as it works for you. He also says that you need not worry as much about structure (lying down is fine). As long as you are making time to go inward and sitting with yourself in silence, you will begin to enjoy the benefits—and this is from the guy who originally invented (while working at the Chopra Wellness Center) the twenty-one-day meditation challenge that Oprah and Deepak facilitate to millions on a regular basis today.

It's important, perhaps, that I tell you what meditation means to me. For me, meditation means giving yourself a break in a world where breaks are rare and demands are never-ending. It means sitting still long enough (daily preferably) for your mind to slow down; it may take some time for that to happen.

I have discovered you will begin to enjoy the benefits by simply making the time to sit still regularly, even at times when your mind is racing (which it will be most of the time). For many, I might add, the best structure seems to be practicing stillness in the morning and before bedtime, but again, no firm structure is required.

For some, like my girlfriend, who find sitting in quiet stillness difficult, practicing guided meditation (being guided by a voice into and during your practice) works well. This is how my girlfriend discovered davidji in the first place, through his guided meditation practice—but, again, it's more important to practice in the way that suits you best.

The benefits of meditation are plenty: less anxiety, more focus, and stronger disease immunity. You can see seventy-six scientific benefits at http:// liveanddare. com/benefits-of-meditation/, but, to me, the greatest benefit is having more abundance of time and overall happiness.

Now, it may sound counter to what you would think, but the more time I spend meditating, the more I am able to accomplish. In interviews with top achievers, I have discovered that I am not alone. In fact, when you start to realize that rock stars, like James Hetfield of Metallica and Paul McCartney; actors, like Clint Eastwood, Jerry Seinfeld, and Nicole Kidman; thought leaders, like Jack Canfield, Dr. John Izzo, Mark Victor Hansen, Oprah, and Deepak Chopra; and mothers and fathers everywhere meditate daily and, in most cases, with great success, isn't that enough to make you want to give it another try, add a bit more meditation to your current practice, add an evening or morning practice, or just keep making time for it?

Yoga

The first time I tried yoga, I was in a room with seventy-five women. I recall my coworkers laughing about my decision to give yoga a try; they asked if I was planning to wear my pink tights. I countered that I was more than happy, being single at the time, to spend an evening with seventy-five women while my coworkers sat at home watching football.

Since then, I have practiced yoga regularly, and much like with meditation, I have been able to better focus as a result of my practice. I have also been able to crush my goals much more quickly. I am more flexible and healthy, emotionally and physically, than I was in my mid-twenties. In fact, I couldn't do these headstand or a reverse downward dog in my mid-twenties, yet here I am at forty doing just that.

Tony Horton, creator of the P90X fitness series, has made yoga a staple of his results-driven programs, and when I asked him about the benefits of yoga, he couldn't have made it more clear that yoga isn't just for relaxation. In fact, he described it as fundamental, one of the most important components of a program that has, perhaps, created more six-packs than any other. Trish Stratus also shared with us that yoga has gotten her into better shape than years of weight training and wrestling.

Hall of fame wrestler Jake "The Snake" Roberts told me that DDP yoga (a form of yoga taught by another well-known wrestler) was one of the core elements that helped him become and remain sober in his late fifties. It helped him put to rest many demons that had plagued him for years and got him into, arguably, his best shape in over twenty years.

Yoga, like meditation, could be a transformational self-care practice for you. For entrepreneurs, in particular, yoga and meditation have been proven to enhance focus, increase productivity, boost energy, battle stress, and improve sleep. Maybe it's time to buy a yoga mat or get yours back out.

Now that we've reached the end of the section on self-care, I challenge you to an exercise. I simply want you to take a few minutes to write out the things you are grateful for at this moment in your life. It can be as simple as writing, "Today, I am grateful for . . ." The bigger challenge, and one I highly recommend, is to pick up a special journal where you can write your gratitude list daily.

Your list can be a specific number. It can be the small things you are grateful for or the big ones. For example, it could simply be that you are grateful you woke up this morning or that you have the ability to wash dishes, which means you have food to cook and eat. It could be a bigger item, like your career. Writing this list for twenty-one to sixty-six days will cement a habit that could easily change your life, according to the work of Maxwell Maltz and the book The One Thing by Gary W. Keller and Jay Papasan

When we review our gratitude list regularly, we begin to see that the few things that may seem like major challenges may not be as important as all we have to be grateful for. Once you've gotten into the habit of writing this list, you begin to see how grateful you truly are for all of the things you have in your life, and my hope is you may realize there are many who are not as fortunate.

The second quick challenge I'd like to see you take is to make your own list of the ways you can serve or give back to others. Some ways I can serve others include the following:

_____

_____

_____

_____

_____

Step 3

IF YOU WANT MORE, GIVE MORE

The third step to becoming more enlightened is to understand the importance of giving.

One action you can take to bring more abundance into your life is by surrounding yourself with people who can give you new ideas, who you can give new ideas to, and who can join you in a collaboration on your journey toward purpose. It's important to note that giving more doesn't have to be related to material or financial wealth; it can be related to things like relationships, love, happiness, knowledge, and the like.

As a general rule, in an equal partnership, you want to bring abundance to one another by each bringing unique strengths. At a bare minimum, you may want to take the advice of our good friend Tony Gambone, founder of the Tough Talk Radio Network: "If you're the smartest person in a room, you need to get out of that room and into a different one."

You may find it strange that I started this section with talk about partnerships. This was intentional. I feel we too often compete with those with whom we could actually collaborate because we operate out of a mindset of scarcity. In other words, we are scared to give because we think it may mean we have to sacrifice something.

My experience during my career and in conversation with many of the world's top thought leaders demonstrates that this couldn't be further from the truth. There is, in fact, so much abundance to be shared that we can have more abundance by working with someone else to create a bigger pie than we can by competing with them for a smaller piece of a smaller pie.

To take this a step further, I recently found myself at a First Nations powwow. A comment I heard during the powwow sums up my feelings on abundance: "There is more than enough to go around, collaboration is much more valuable and powerful than competition."

Another comment at the powwow struck me as particularly insightful: "We have a belief in our culture about giving—it states that what you give comes back to you at least tenfold." They made this comment while sending a blanket around the powwow circle so that anyone who wanted to give, and could do so, had a way to give some money to help a little girl who had hurt her leg while dancing. If they wanted to give, they could simply place some money on the blanket. For me, it was a powerful visual experience.

Consider, if you will, the partnership between W. Clement Stone and Napoleon Hill. Hill was the celebrated author of the landmark 1930s bestseller *Think and Grow Rich,* a book that has been said to have motivated more people than any other book in history to make massive changes in their personal and professional lives. *Think and Grow Rich* was based on more than twenty-five years of research into the habits of the greatest thought leaders of Hill's time.

W. Clement Stone was the founder of a major insurance company. Stone met Hill when Hill was semi-retired, and Stone convinced him to come out of retirement so together they could write the powerful book *Success through a Positive Mental Attitude* (PMA) and Hill could continue his lectures across the nation. Hill's impact may, in fact, be immeasurable. This is the power of giving.

Two of our previous show guests, Jack Canfield and Mark Victor Hansen, were competitors in the speaking industry who came together and once again proved we can have fruitful partnerships with people who would otherwise be competitors. They realized the power of giving. As a result of having this giving belief (that if you give, it will come back many times over), they tied a donation directly to the sales of the Chicken Soup book series.

The series has since sold five hundred million copies, and a percentage of their sales has been donated to causes they believe in. Now, it's worth noting, they weren't planning to give simply so they would receive, but based on core numbers alone, I think we can say that is exactly what happened. Not surprisingly perhaps, Jack and Mark actually tie a donation to all projects they are involved in.

Just consider the invisible impact these two tithers have had on the world. I think we can say their collaboration didn't negatively impact the pies they were each competing for. Instead, they built a much bigger pie together, which, in turn, allowed them to give much more back to society than they otherwise could have alone. I think you'll find this is a common belief in enlightened circles, but sadly, it is not yet a common belief (or practice) for the majority.

So, if there is enough abundance for everyone, it stands to reason that multiple people working toward their goals will result in greater outcomes for everyone than each person working on their own. At the same time, these collaborators will not impede one another's results, since there isn't a scarce amount of success (or whatever you're looking for).

I believe becoming more enlightened can be achieved by finding ways to work with others (especially those you normally wouldn't work with) toward a common goal, as this can raise your awareness of new ideas, bolster your efforts, and teach you how to execute in new ways. In fact, you both bring personal experiences to the mix, and you may have access to each other's networks. These factors help grow the overall pie. Now, it's important to note you have to be open-minded during this process for it to have any real chance for success.

At this point, you may be asking yourself, "How does someone start the process of working with others toward a common goal so that together you can grow a bigger pie?" First, you have to decide with whom you'd like to work and why. I recommend you start by grabbing a pen and a piece of paper. Of course, you can use a computer or phone if you'd like, but personally, I like the old-school route when it comes to lists.

Once you have your selected recording tool, you simply start building a list of the people you feel you are aligned with: people who share your beliefs, who have a similar level of passion, who have the same level of integrity. You can draw your list from your social media contacts, groups, networks, or introductions from those you trust.

When you have the list of potential partners ready, it's time to map out the ways in which you could effectively work with each person. Also, you want to make sure each partnership will take you closer to your goals and purpose.

You'll also want to decide how much time you have to dedicate to partnerships because having too many partnerships may detract from the results you are working toward.

Depending on your industry, your schedule or the structure of the partnership (business partnership or mentorship), you may have time for just one partnership. As long as it's a partnership aligned with your goals and purpose, one is plenty.

For the first two years of our radio show, my business partner and producer was a gentleman named Marco Kelly. I could not have launched the show or grown it to a top-rated show on iTunes (another partnership of mine) without my partnership with Marco.

So far, you've recorded a list of potential partners, decided who aligns with your goals/purpose, and considered how much time you have to dedicate to partnerships. That means it's time to reach out to some potential partners to see who may be open to collaboration.

Giving and Receiving

A couple of years ago, I interviewed seasoned networker and politician Matt Whitman. When I asked him about the importance of giving back, he noted one way he became enlightened years before. It was the day he realized he had spent the first twenty years of his life focused on himself; he decided he wanted to spend the next twenty years (and the rest of his life, in fact) focusing on others.

He added a quote that a friend of his shared with him years earlier to describe how he spends his life now: "If you want more love, give more love." This is one quotation where we can change the main word to almost any area of our life. For instance, "If you want more hugs, give more hugs"; "If you want more peace, give more peace"; and, on the other side, "If you want more hate, give more hate."

The message is clear: Matt has discovered that spending his time giving brings him much more joy (and, dare I say, purpose) than taking.

I mentioned earlier that many enlightened individuals have learned that when they give, it comes back many times over. I'd also like to add that giving equals happiness. There are countless articles that back this up. In fact, you can read one right here based on psychology: https://www.psychologytoday.com/ blog/ out-the-darkness/201501/happiness-comes-giving-not-buying- and-having.

On our radio show, we regularly talk with enlightened super-achievers about the importance and power of being of service to others. Not surprisingly, the vast majority of our guests believe in the power of being of service, and they spend a large majority of their time doing so.

Like the article above notes, these super-achievers also believe serving others enhances their own well-being and provides optimal levels of happiness—even though they are often making a difference in the lives of many others in the process of serving.

The important thing here is that, of course, they are doing it for the right reasons. For instance, Anthony Robbins, world-renowned speaker, author, and peak performance strategist, not only donated his advance and all of the proceeds of his recent book *Money: Master the Game* to Feeding America, which helps feed millions of people across the country, but he has also personally brought buses of people to inner cities each Christmas season to hand out meals to the homeless.

He gives as a result of an experience he had as a child when someone gave to him and his family during a time of need. I'm certain that Robbins receives as much as he gives. Perhaps this plays a big part in his energy level and ability to smile every day while he maintains his demanding schedule.

Someone I have known well for some time has been retired for years, and every time I see him, he doesn't appear to have aged. He also always has a genuine smile on his face. Many people seem to lose their way after retiring. Not him. Why? I think it has a large part to do with the fact he volunteers and serves so many on a regular basis. His purpose (and perhaps passion) has been that of helping others in need. It has, perhaps, been the natural medicine that keeps him young.

Further, I have some people in my life who are in recovery from the disease of addiction. I have attended a few Alcoholics Anonymous (AA) meetings in the last year to support them and their recovery. I have been simply blown away by the extent to which many in the AA program serve and support one another. In fact, I learned of the word "altruistic" as a result of AA, and I have tried to further incorporate it into my life on a regular basis.

I could provide example after example of people who are helping others and who are, at the same time, among the most purposeful and sometimes happy people you will ever meet. It is important to serve, give back, and donate. Once you find the way that feels right and works best for you, you will discover the many ways serving others will, in turn, improve your own well-being and happiness.

I would like to leave you with the following thought in the area of giving and receiving and perhaps help you to determine ways you can baby step into the world of giving, if it's not something you are currently accustomed to.

The thought I'd like to leave you with is this: the better you are at giving *and* receiving (one without the other means a lack of balance), the more fulfillment you will ultimately enjoy. That's a bold statement but one that I have seen proven time and again during so many conversations with enlightened super-achievers.

The great part is, the giving doesn't have to be money. It doesn't have to be grandiose and frequent. Giving your time or knowledge can be more valuable and make a bigger impact many times than the giving of money.

So, now is a great time to grab a fresh cup of coffee or a smoothie and a fresh piece of paper or your journal write down ways you can start giving (time, money, resources, and so on). I offer a prompt below for you to complete.

I can give the following as a way of showing appreciation for the life I have:

_____

_____

_____

_____

_____

_____

On the other side of things, many find it easy to give but difficult to receive. If that is the case for you, now is a great time, while you're sipping your coffee or drinking that smoothie, to think of the reasons why you find it so difficult to receive. In many cases, knowing the cause can help you find the solution. You may have to go really deep with this one, and you may not find the answer right away. It may mean looking at your past. Even so, it's still worth the effort because you're absolutely worthy of receiving all that you deserve. In other words, you are worth it!

Here is some space to record your thoughts on receiving. An example could be, "The reason I have trouble receiving is because my culture has always said it is far better to give than receive."

The reason I have trouble receiving is the following:

_____

_____

_____

_____

_____

_____

Step 4

THE BETTER-LIFE FORMULA REVEALED

M ost of us realize the power that negative and positive energy have on our life. It is my belief that negative energy is at the root of many dis-eases, that it is, in fact, negative energy that causes our bodies to disintegrate toward dis-ease.

I have mentioned W. Clement Stone and Napoleon Hill and their life-changing book *Success through a Positive Mental Attitude*. In the book, they talk about Positive Mental Attitude (PMA) and Negative Mental Attitude (NMA). They share their belief that living with a PMA and avoiding a NMA can be the difference between living a fulfilling and prosperous life or one filled with negativity, despair, and (often) disease. They go on to say the law states that we translate into physical reality the thoughts and attitudes we hold in our mind, no matter what those thoughts and attitudes are.

Another culture that believes in the power of energy is the First Nations culture. In fact, they believe negative energy has so much power that before they enter a sweat lodge, each person has to be smudged (cleansed/cleared) of negativity. It's so important in some tribes that during my first sweat, when I left the lodge and tried to come back in without smudging, everyone had to come back out and re-smudge. The belief was, I might bring negative energy back in with me.

If you doubt the power of negative energy, consider a dog who is friendly with everyone, but when a certain person enters your house, the dog doesn't want that person anywhere nearby. That dog is, no doubt, picking up an energy that we have not sensed. Consider as well the times when you are in a place, someone walks in, and the entire energy of the room changes.

To further demonstrate this point about the power of negative energy, I would like to share a personal experience. When I was nineteen, I moved across the country from a town with a population of just five thousand and began working in a city with a population of close to one million people. Within no time, I was thriving in my career but struggling in my personal life. I had never been around so many people before, and soon I found myself battling generalized anxiety.

Within short order, I was visiting local medical centers and spending time in their waiting rooms. It was a wonder I didn't have my own coffee mug; I had become such a regular. Soon my anxiety escalated to a point where, eventually, every time I read about a disease, I began to develop the symptoms. If I thought anxiety was bad, I had no idea what I would face with hypochondria (abnormal anxiety about health or unwarranted fear of having a serious disease).

Now, saddled with hypochondria, I wasn't just spending time in waiting rooms. I was getting booked for MRIs, EKGs, and X-rays to try and determine what disease I had—when, in fact, the disease itself was hypochondria.

Of course, no actual disease was found because there was no disease to find other than the disease of thinking I had a disease. I know; it sounds like a riddle!

Each time I was about to settle on the fact that it was all in my mind, I would read about another disease, and then, ta-da, the cycle would begin again. This continued for years. This is the power of negative energy. But, the good news is that positive energy is just as powerful.

Positive energy was powerful enough to bring me out of my negative energy phase. All I had to do to tap into it was uncover my passion. Consider the difference in me today after having uncovered my passion in my mid-twenties.

When I discovered my passion and PMA, my somewhat lengthy battle with hypochondria and anxiety officially ended.

So, how can you become more enlightened as it relates to energy? How can you bring more positive energy into your life while removing some of the negative energy at the same time?

First, you have to take action. What should that action look like? A good starting point is to take an inventory of the aspects of your life that involve negative energy and the aspects that involve positive energy so you know what to remove and what to add. the worksheets at the end of this section should help you identify and remove some of your negative energy as you build more of the positive energy.

First let's start with positive. In terms of positive energy, let me first say that, as was described by Napoleon Hill many years ago, "Thoughts become things." Hill described this further with his powerful quote, "Whatever the man of mind can conceive and believe, he can achieve."

Christine Campbell, a great Canadian musician, dreamed of opening for the legendary performer Bob Seger. In 2014, the opportunity presented itself. Seger was coming to town, and the promoter was looking for an opening act. Christine took action by letting people know she was interested.

Bigger, though, than the action she took in a public capacity, Christine used her mind and, therefore, the power of positive energy to help seal the deal. As she explained, "Every morning and every night, leading up to the event, I got up in the morning and said, 'I'm so excited to be opening for Seger today.' I put the positive energy, and my intention, out there."

Did it work? In 2014, despite massive competition from many well-established artists, Christine found herself opening for Bob Seger, not just once but twice.

Each day, Christine practiced what is described in another powerful quote by the late Norman Vincent Peale: "You can bring about the ideal condition by persistently acting as though the ideal condition already exists." Christine acted as though the condition existed, and within short order, it did exist. This happens every single day in the world of business and life, and it can work for you as well.

Leading up to my *Enlightened* book's release, I said an affirmation every day that "more than fifteen thousand people grabbed a copy of the book in the first two months of the book's launch." I said this affirmation as if it had already occurred. I said, "I am so excited that more than fifteen thousand people have grabbed a copy of the new *Enlightened* book in February 2016." This was my twice-daily affirmation.

What will yours be? Feel free to use the applicable spot at the end of this section to put your affirmation together.

An element you may want to consider is using our process (the one we provided earlier) for identifying your passion and purpose. If you haven't yet done so, identifying your passion and purpose will add to your balance of positive energy.

I have another exercise for you. I think it's a great time for you to compare the ways you are bringing negative energy into your life with the ways you are bringing positive energy into your life. This exercise will help you see where you currently stand and where changes may be required. For instance, if you have a heavy negative list and light positive list, you are going to run into some major challenges in your effort to be a positive person.

As an example, you may note in the negative behavior section that the way you are engaging in negative behavior is that you complain every morning that you have to get up and go to work. In the "how you can change this" (replacement behavior) section, you may note that you can make a work-related gratitude list as soon as you wake up each day and then spend fifteen minutes doing something you love before you start getting ready for work.

Do you have your pen ready? OK, here goes. Ways I am engaging in negative behavior and ways I can work at changing that negative behavior include the following:

Negative Behavior	Replacement Behavior

Ways I am engaging in positive behavior and more ways I can engage in positive behavior include the following:

Existing Positive Behavior	New Positive Behavior

This exercise should give you a strong idea of where you stand and where you could make changes. If you are having trouble coming up with ideas for how you can bring more positive energy into your life through positive behavioral practices, here are some ideas:

- Practicing yoga
- Exercising
- Reading positive material (books, posts, and blogs)
- Attending positivity seminars

- Listening to positive audio recordings
- Reading positive quotes
- Meditating
- Attending a concert by a band you enjoy
- Attending a stand-up comedy show

Step 5

WHAT DO THE LEADERS OF YESTERDAY HAVE IN COMMON?

We had Dr. John Izzo on our radio show recently, and shortly after, I found myself re-listening to his great audio book *The Five Secrets You Must Discover before You Die*. In the book, he talks in-depth about the sad fact that we, in North America, don't see the value in learning from the elderly like other cultures do.

I mentioned First Nations' traditions earlier, and I have learned so much in a short time from the elders within the sweat lodges and powwows I've attended. I am still amazed at how much respect there is for the elders within First Nations' culture.

Typically, an elder leads the sweat, shares the knowledge, and does the storytelling; everyone is hanging on his every word. During feasts, elders (and children) eat first and get the choice seating spots.

In essence, elders are revered in some cultures, whereas in the majority of cases in North America, we are so busy being busy that we don't feel we have time to learn from our elders. We simply place them in manors or long-term care facilities, and their knowledge is lost with them. We barely visit these facilities or the elders within their walls because we are so busy, busy, busy.

There is some good news, however. In one circle I am familiar with in North America, elders have always been, and continue to be, revered. This circle is the "thought leadership" circle. In the thought leadership world, these leaders (otherwise known as the leaders of the personal/professional development game) are sought out for their knowledge and wisdom.

Consider the late Zig Ziglar, a top trainer and speaker in the thought leadership world. At age eighty-four, he developed short-term memory loss from a fall down a flight of stairs, but upwards of fifteen thousand people at a time were paying to attend his seminars.

We even sought out his knowledge for our business publication, and the knowledge he shared during our interview still stands against any interview we have conducted. Even now, years after Ziglar's passing, his Facebook following has grown from hundreds of thousands to over three million followers.

Leaders still with us, like Wayne Dyer and Deepak Chopra, have people extremely excited to attend their events and hanging onto their every word. (Editor's note: Wayne Dyer was still alive when I wrote this portion, but he has since passed. I attended his Hay House tribute event in Orlando, and I have even more respect now than ever for the man affectionately known as the "Father of Motivation.")

The students of such leaders are, in many cases, becoming the leaders of today. Why? Because they value the wisdom and knowledge of their elders in the thought leadership world and find the time to seek out such wisdom in this busy, busy world.

We recently had Don Miguel Ruiz Jr., who wrote *The Five Levels of Attachment*, on our show again. His family has continued to share Toltec wisdom generation after generation, and the elders sharing the wisdom are revered. His father, who brought us *The Four Agreements*, taught Toltec wisdom to his son. Soon, his father is retiring, and Don Miguel Ruiz Jr. will be slowing down to care for and continue to learn from his father. This demonstrates how much they revere the wisdom of elders in their circle. What can we learn from this?

If the elders in the thought leadership game, the Ruiz family, and cultures around the world can be sought for their wisdom and knowledge and the result is that traditions (and fundamental success and fulfilment principles) survive thousands of years, doesn't it stand to reason that we would be further ahead if we tried to learn from the minds of so many who have gone before on the rough roads we are currently travelling? The result could be new enlightened leaders emerging to take over where the late great leaders left off.

The fundamentals and principles of personal and professional success haven't changed as much as you might think. In fact, Napoleon Hill studied hundreds of millionaires over a twenty-five-year period in the 1920s and 30s and shared the findings in the landmark book *Think and Grow Rich*. In recent years, I have interviewed more people than Hill profiled in his book, and the principles and fundamentals of personal and professional success, in large part, haven't changed.

How can we start putting more focus on the elders in our lives and the wisdom and knowledge they can share with us? A great starting point is understanding that anyone who can teach us something we don't know (meaning anyone who has gained wisdom by trial and error or from wisdom shared with them) is truly an elder.

Perhaps the best way you can show respect for the wisdom obtained by others is to develop a learning plan that encourages you to learn from others regularly. The days we have the option of learning on demand, something previous generations never had. Whether that learning is via podcasts, videos (think TED Talks or YouTube), magazines, books, audio interviews, or even social media, we can select and pick our learning sources in advance.

Then we can have the learning come to us right as we're ready for it, rather than having to wait until that one time a week when a specific program starts on cable TV. There is more content online than we can absorb and execute in our entire lives.

That's the good news, but the good news, of course, comes with some challenges. The new challenge is choosing your sources wisely and remaining focused on the few, rather than the many, sources that can provide the specific wisdom you are looking for.

I also mentioned earlier that we are now in an information-heavy and wisdom-light world. Your success in the years to come will be in discovering the right sources and learning from them regularly, rather than sifting through all of the information that bombards you on a daily basis.

This is, perhaps, a great time to discuss designing and developing your *learning plan* so that you, too, can avoid the "get lost in the information" challenge many of us face. Designing and developing an effective learning plan involves answering some key questions:

In what formats do you learn best?

Audio _____

Visual _____

Print _____

What type of wisdom do you require?

Soft (customer service, sales, etc.) Skills _____

Technical (industry specific, trade) Skills _____

What learning sources fit your lifestyle/learning style?

Podcasts _____

Books _____

Magazines _____

Video _____

Apps _____

Mentors _____

Seminars (Live Events) _____

How much time can you dedicate to learning (per week)?

One Hour _____

Two Hours _____

Three Hours _____

More _____

Consider the people you admire. What titles are they reading? Who are they listening to and watching?

Reading _____

Listening to _____

Watching _____

If I answered these questions, here is a sample of what I could have come up with: audio, visual, and print; I'm looking for soft skills (non-technical, industry-specific skills). I prefer podcasts, books, and mentors. I can allocate a minimum of three hours per week (a little over thirty minutes each day) to learning. The people I admire (I can base this one on our interviews with top achievers) are reading books like *Think and Grow Rich* and *How to Win Friends and Influence People*, listening to podcasts like *Entrepreneur on Fire,* and watching TED Talks.

As a result, I can determine a learning plan that could include watching a TED Talk three days a week (perhaps Monday, Wednesday, and Friday), reading for fifteen minutes each day from books my mentors read (e.g., *Think and Grow Rich*, *The Compound Effect)* or a magazine like *Success* (which also provides lists of books that achievers read), and listening to a podcast like *Entrepreneur on Fire* on Tuesdays and Thursdays.

I should note this is, in fact, similar to my current learning plan. Here is the amazing part. If I listen to the podcasts while driving to meetings, watch TEDx Talks while eating my breakfast, and read for just fifteen minutes before I kick into my work, I can add 144 hours per year (or almost a full month of dedicated learning) to my personal and professional development without impacting my life in a major way.

What does your learning plan look like?

Mentorship

Another important part of your learning plan will be the mentors who enter your life. The great part is that your mentor program can be as formal or informal as you choose. It can be as simple as making a list of the people you would like to learn from and inviting one per week out to dinner, reading their books, watching their videos, or approaching them and together coming up with a mentorship schedule (perhaps an hour a week or twice a week) in which you will map out strategies for your life and career. These strategy-making sessions could include creating goals, targets, measurement tools, a task list, and more.

In any case, it's important to select the right mentors to meet your needs. This may be a good time to make a list of the people you would like to have as mentors so you can begin reaching out.

People I would like to be mentored by include the following:

———————————————————————————————————

———————————————————————————————————

———————————————————————————————————

———————————————————————————————————

———————————————————————————————————

As a final note on learning, whatever amount of time you dedicate, you should always be on the hunt for other ways in which you can grow and learn. For example, my girlfriend and I recently watched *Enter the Dragon* starring Bruce Lee. I'm a Bruce Lee fan and have been since I was a little tyke. In addition to enjoying the action in his movies, I feel inspired by his quotes and philosophies. After watching the bonus footage (including interviews with Bruce), my girlfriend became intrigued by some of his insight, and we found ourselves reflecting on his wisdom and discussing some of his quotes.

It turns out, even an evening with a Bruce Lee movie can be an opportunity to expand your learning. Here are just three of Bruce's quotes we discussed during our two hours of mind expansion:

"I fear not the man who has practiced 10,000 kicks once, but I fear the man who has practiced one kick 10,000 times." This quote relates so well to the ten-thousand-hour rule I reflected on earlier.

"If you spend too much time thinking about a thing, you'll never get it done." This quote relates to my talk on The Law of Action and how practicing it might just be more important than The Law of Attraction.

"A goal is not always meant to be reached; it often serves simply as something to aim at." In our interview with Jack Canfield, he talked about how he and his wife set a goal to achieve one hundred thousand dollars in sales the year after hitting just eight thousand dollars. He ended up achieving ninety-three thousand. Many told him they were sorry he didn't achieve his goal, perhaps missing the point that he almost made ten times his income simply by setting a goal. To me, this exemplifies Bruce's quote nicely.

Not a bad amount of reflection and learning simply because I convinced my girlfriend to watch *Enter The Dragon* with me, is it?

Step 6

IT'S NOT ABOUT WHAT PEOPLE SAY WHEN YOU'RE AROUND; IT'S WHAT THEY SAY WHEN YOU'RE NOT AROUND

I t can take years to build a legacy that makes you proud and only minutes to create a legacy that embarrasses you. Consider the recent cases of Harvey Weinstein and Bill Cosby.

Building a legacy you can be proud of impacts every part of your life. My grandfather, a carpenter with a grade 3 education, built a fiberglass space shuttle replica when I was just seven years of age. He was even told that his ability to work with blueprints was beyond that of many professional engineers and architects. Until the day he died, anytime anyone asked if he actually built that shuttle, he brimmed with pride. That shuttle, which still stands some thirty years later, became part of his legacy. Further, for me, his legacy and gift was showing me that nothing is impossible if we step outside our comfort zones long enough to experience it.

Having the right legacy while you're still alive can create trust among the people in your personal and professional life. The right legacy also helps you to determine what you should say yes and no to each day. Therefore, your legacy has as much impact on your productivity as anything else you do. The right legacy can mean *living on purpose rather than living someone else's purpose.*

This is why understanding your legacy results in enlightenment and individual growth. If you know your passion and purpose and live your purpose regularly, your legacy will often be within sight.

In Don Miguel Ruiz's landmark book, *The Four Agreements*, he talks about four agreements you should make with yourself if you want to live a fulfilled and meaningful life. If you practice agreement 1, being impeccable with your word, your legacy in the area of trust will be among the highest of levels.

Stephen M. R. Covey told me when we met in Alberta, Canada, a couple of years back that trust is everything. His bestselling book *Trust* echoes this statement and expands upon it in great detail.

In the first and third Acts of this book, I revealed that my personal mission statement is "To be known as the guy who donated, motivated, entertained, educated, and inspired." As long as what I'm doing at any given time is bringing me closer to that mission and purpose, I know I'm spending my time in the right places and building the right legacy.

Determining your own passion + purpose statement will help you make decisions about your time. It will enable you to ask yourself if any given task brings you closer to your purpose and hits the key areas of your passion + purpose statement.

As you work toward building your legacy, this mission statement will guide you and ensure you will be proud of what you leave behind. Your legacy will also ensure you make an impact on others while you're here and hopefully long after you're gone. And just consider the visible/invisible impact you could have if you live a life aligned with your true purpose.

Consider this: my girlfriend and I recently embarked on our Invisible Impact Tour that included twenty-six states and five provinces in sixteen days. During the tour, we visited Jimi Hendrix's gravesite in Seattle. In just one hour, we witnessed four groups of people visit his memorial site and take photos. We talked about what Hendrix meant to them. I suspect at least one group must visit his memorial site every day.

But it gets bigger. While we were there, a gentleman pulled up in a little red car and jumped out. He had rubber gloves on, and he made his way around the memorial site, picking up garbage. He then got back into his car and drove off.

It's doubtful he works for the graveyard since he only cleaned one site. I think it's a fair guess he probably lives nearby and drops by to clean Hendrix's site regularly.

Do you think Hendrix had a major invisible impact on this gentleman? I think it's safe to say yes. Did I forget to mention that Hendrix has been dead for forty-five years? This is simply a small part of his legacy. Being aligned with your purpose and building the right legacy can mean the difference between having that kind of impact and walking around like a working zombie each day.

Your legacy doesn't have to be the result of grandiose acts. One of my former teacher's actions had a profound impact on me and influenced who I am. I'm quite certain she had the same impact on many other students over the years; that is perhaps her legacy, both today and tomorrow. She may not have written a passion + purpose statement, but she has built a powerful legacy just the same. That said, why leave it to chance (or accident) when you can determine now what you'd like your legacy to be and take action steps to direct it?

So, with that, rewrite your passion + purpose statement here so we can make sure you're building the right legacy now. My purpose statement (the one you wrote in Step 1) is as follows:

_____

_____

_____

_____

_____

_____

With your purpose statement at hand, now it's time to write down the ways it can have an impact (visible or invisible) on others and the world. Again, remember it doesn't have to be grandiose. An example from my life could be the following: my name is Corey Poirier; my passion is speaking to audiences about passion, purpose, legacy, and customer service; and my purpose is to inspire, motivate, donate, entertain, and educate.

Next, let me share an example of the ways my purpose could impact others: I may inspire someone to find or begin pursuing their passion. This will not only result in their happiness but ripple and impact others in a bigger way. I may entertain someone and allow them to escape for an hour or so, and this could allow them to get outside of themselves and forget their troubles or provide them with a memory worth sharing. I may give back to someone (donate), not realizing just how much they really needed the help. This, in turn, could empower them to find ways they can pay it forward.

So, with that in mind, it's your turn. My purpose statement (the one you just wrote above) is as follows:

_____
_____
_____
_____
_____
_____

Ways that my purpose can impact others include the following:

_____
_____
_____
_____
_____

There you have it, Act 3 of *The Book of Why (and How)*. I hope this book (and the upcoming bonus section) helps you reach every single one of your goals while also helping you take your personal and professional life to a whole new level. We're looking forward to hearing all about your results in the coming months and years.

Next Steps

You may be wondering what the next step should be. You may be thinking, where do I go from here?

To me, it all starts with action. One my of favorite quotes is, "You don't have to be great to start, but you do have to start to be great." (I've seen this one credited to both Zig Ziglar and Les Brown, so perhaps I'll give both of them credit here).

For your next step, I'd love to see you take some action, any action, so that you begin to build your momentum. As far as what step to take next, here are a few options to consider.

Option 1: Get Access to the Bonus Material

I've mentioned elsewhere that I have some bonus material available for you. If you want to access that material, just visit www.coreypoirier.ca and select "Bonus Material," and you'll be all set.

Option 2: Join Our New Membership Tribe

If you love what you've learned in this book but you're a business owner or entrepreneur who likes to dive deep, take action, learn visually (video training), collaborate with others, and more, perhaps you'd like to check out our membership program in which you'll learn more about how to regularly attract client leads, increase media and brand visibility, and become an influencer (perhaps by speaking from a stage), or write and release your first book. Learn more at www.coreypoirier.ca under the "Membership Tribe" section.

Option 3: Bring Corey in to Speak at Your Event

If you feel I might be a good fit for your event and would like to learn more about bringing me in to speak at your event and/or work with your team, feel free to visit www.thatspeakerguy.com and/or reach out at conversationswithleaders@gmail.com.

Option 4: Learn More about Speaking from the Stage for High Fees And High Impact

If you've ever had a desire to speak from the stage, perhaps for impact or high fees, our Speaking Program may be of interest. You can learn more (and check out some free video training) at www. thespeakingprogram.com. If you want to be added to the waiting list for the next time the program opens, just send an email along to conversationswithleaders@gmail.com

ABOUT THE AUTHOR

Corey Poirier is an award-winning keynote speaker, multiple-time TEDx, PMx, and MoMondays speaker. He is also the host of the top-rated *Conversations With PASSION* radio show and a newer, top-rated speaking-related podcast, *The Speaking Program*. He has been featured in one-hour television specials on Eastlink TV and TeleTelevision and is a columnist with *Entrepreneur* and *Forbes*.

A member of the Forbes Coaches Council, he has also appeared or been featured in Global TV, CBS, CTV, NBC, ABC, CBC TV, and Second City and is one of the few leaders featured twice on the popular *Entrepreneur on Fire* show.

He has interviewed over four thousand of the world's top leaders in search of success traits, and he is a father, boyfriend, yogi, stand-up comedian, and musician who has skydived—despite a fear of heights—surfed in Tofino, British Columbia, and Snorkeled in Key West, despite an inability to swim.

You can find him regularly finding new ways to expand his comfort zone in various places through the world.

Bonus Section

QUOTES TO LIVE AND LEARN BY

"To seek a life of great influence and contribution, one must risk ridicule and rejection by deciding to be heard, often in the face of resistance and conformity."
—**Allan Wich,** Exponential Growth Consultant and
CEO of The Wich Group, Co-Host of *Think Bold Be Bold* Radio

"Harmony, melodious music calls me ever deeper. I play my inner song and join in the choir of nature, finding my notes blend with those all around me, soaring in harmony with Mother Earth."
— **Ellen Carey**, Thought Leader

"My imperfections are my abilities, as my disabilities are my perfections."
— **Henry Joey Poirier**, Holistic Artist

"Going after your dream will require hard work, determination, and sacrifices. Are you willing to do it and still maintain a balanced life?"
— **Alicja B. Lombard**, Gypsy Owl Productions

"Want to make a positive difference in today's world? Compliment someone on their smile, their eyes, their shoes. Tell a silly joke; hold the door and say 'after you'; pay for their cup of coffee or other random act of kindness. Spreading joy to others heals not only their soul but uplifts yours as well."

— **Alicia White**, Back of the Room Productions

"When you can discover how to 'let go,' you will have the key to happiness."

— **Mary Ellen Ciganovich**, Inspirational Speaker, Author

"When you frequently and consistently add value to others without expectation of reward or compensation, there is potential for positive things in your career to happen."

— **Brian Hill**, Owner/Director of Training, Mental Ammo

"Live from your heart, that you may know the fullness of Life and the sweetness of Love."

— **Jeanine DuBois**, Compassion's Doorway

"When you love someone with an addiction, an important part of the healing journey is to grieve for what has been lost and for what will never be. Beautiful freedom awaits."

— **Charmaine Quintana**

"There's always time to be nice to someone. This will be your biggest 'impact' in everything you do."

— **Brenda Powell**, Research Associate

"When you distinguish what you do, what you do becomes knowledge. When you distinguish what you know, what you know becomes wisdom. When you distinguish your wisdom, you are living it."

— **Dianne Collins**, Creator of QuantumThink, Author of
Do You QuantumThink? New Thinking That Will Rock Your World

"When you know who you are, you will know what you want, and then you will know where you are going in life."
— **Christopher Cumby**, Sales Success Coach, Sales Consultant, Author and Speaker, Founder of Success Playbook and Integrity Marketing Inc., Host of *Think Bold, Be Bold*

"There's always hope; sometimes it's just hidden behind fear."
— **Nicky V**, Author and Entrepreneur

"Have the courage to follow your heart. Your heart will never steer you in the wrong direction because it is through your heart that the universe speaks to you. I guarantee that you will find your dream in that place where your mind meets your heart and your soul."
— **Tom Ingrassia**, Founder and President, The MotivAct Group/Tom Ingrassia Productions

"The entire universe and our small planet is meant to grow and thrive. For you to hold back your potential is to go against the natural flow of everything. Live what you dream. Live courageously, and you become the universe."
— **Aaron Law**, The Empowered Farmer, Keynote Speaker, Trainer, and Coach

"It all starts with you and your willingness to pause and say, 'I am going to take back my power.'"
— **Hilde Larsen**, Certified Health and Success Coach, Inspirational Speaker, Detox Specialist, and Author

"Everything happens for a reason! Even if the reason might not seem very clear at first, the important piece is to know that everything in life is happening for us, not to us. Every situation, no matter if it's good or bad, holds a gift that we can learn from."
— **Kay Sanders**, Business Coach and Bestselling Author

"I have a dream of permanently improving the neighborhoods around me by helping 'happy people' find 'happy places' to live. If you help enough people find their 'happy place,' you might just find your own in the process."

— **Jenna Ross**, Happy Place Property Management

"We are past the point of ignoring the importance of retaining good people within our workforce as part of a valid growth strategy. The conventional methods, habits, and thinking that have allowed current businesses to thrive in the last thirty years will simply not be sufficient to grow in the next thirty years. We will not have the large demographic pool going forward to continue enjoying the luxury of a 'revolving door' of attaining positive growth in business. Organizations that dedicate newer attitudes on inspiring talent to stay and develop their skills and those that promote their people's welfare will win in the future marketplaces of the world."

— **Greg Powell**, Financial Center Manager, Sun Life Financial, Surrey

"Life is a journey of the heart; the mind is only a helper, and the soul is the adventurer."

— **Gabriella Guglielminotti Trivel**, Author of *Antarctic Odyssey: A New Beginning*

"Of all things, feelings, and emotions, I found the energy and reach of *love* is essential and all-encompassing. *Loving* yourself and others as yourself lets you express the knowledge that we are all *one in love*. Be kind; encourage each other; help out where you can; and keep on *loving*. True *love* (agape) is the essence and meaning of life. Everything else will follow suit."

— **Dr. Christine Sauer**, Christine's Commonsense Health Coaching Ltd.

"Your situation won't change if you're not willing to change. To change, you need to grow; to grow, you need to challenge yourself; to challenge yourself, you need to take risks; to take risks, you need to get out of your comfort zone."

— **Karen Penton**, District Manager, Independent Consultant at Arbonne

"In my more lucid moments, I try to take myself less seriously and my mission more seriously."

— **Dada Nabhaniilananda**, The Monk Dude

"Whatever you reach for, be enough without it first."

— **Nikki Martin**, Yoga Teacher, Author

"Chasing a dream without putting in the time and hard work is akin to reaching for the stars while sitting on your couch looking out the window. Learning key skills and creating opportunities through networking, long hours, and hard work will land you on the moon each and every time."

— **Drew Carson**, Host of *Terror Firma* Podcast

"The rinse-and-repeat cycle is the ego's natural way to prevent change. The ego tells you that you can't change, thereby creating self- doubt. It tells you that you can't change your current situation or do something new because, if you do, your friends and family will think you have gone bonkers, thus creating fear. This is the rinse-and- repeat cycle of limiting beliefs."

— **Sue P. Singleton**, Certified Coach

"You have to stand up and let the world know how great you are at what you do. If you wait for others to recommend or anoint you as an expert in your field, it may never happen. Don't be afraid to promote yourself to get the opportunities you and your family deserve."

— **Joel Helfer**, AM Talk Radio Producer,
Amazon Bestselling Author, and Speaker

"Happiness cannot be scaled, counted, or compared; it is a way of being."

— **Rhonna del Rio**, Yogi

"Your acts of kindness really do have a ripple effect."

— **Lynda Kaplan**, Author of *Loving Me*

"Stay hungry, but remember to take a bite of life along the way."

— **Kitti McKay**, Owner/Founder/Operator at Kitti Kleen

"The more authentic you become, the more authenticity you create. Be self-full. Trust your own ideas. Be a maverick!!"

— **Jaya Chauhan**, Thought Leader

"Choosing the right business or life partner is a key ingredient for a successful life. Inspirational leaders know how to build their social capital for continued accomplishment and understand that, at the end of the day, relationships matter most."

— **Jennifer B. Rhodes**, PsyD, Licensed Psychologist, Dating Coach, Image Consultant and Founder of Rapport, A Boutique Relationships Agency, LLC

"Use your mindset to serve you in your journey instead of sabotaging your journey."

— **Samantha Bonnell**, Life Enrichment Advisor

"Niche 'til it hurts. Focus on the thing that your company does best, and eliminate all other activities to focus on growing that one thing."

— **Derric Haynie**, CEO at Vulpine Interactive

"In order to make my most impressionable impact on others, to and for the world, I need to be operating from a place of true self-love and wholeness. I can give my best me if I am my best me."

— **Holly Ruttenbur Dickinson**, Author, Homemaker, and Philanthropist

"Man, searching for God, is like a fish, swimming around the ocean, searching for water."

— **Stan-The-HuMan**™

"When will the human race turn toward human kind? When your heart leads your human mind."

— **Tracy Williams-Duerr**, BComm, CPA, CMA Accountant; Face Painter; Community Volunteer; Spiritual Seeker

"Happiness is never driven to look for itself. It is itself. The drive to be self-confident is the continuation of self-doubt. Catch yourself in these conversations with yourself, and before you know it, you'll stop asking yourself for direction because you will believe you are not lost."

— **JoAnn Aparo Neurath**, Founder of Saltcoats, Writer, and Photographer

"Life and leadership are exceedingly simple. Every second of every day, we are choosing between two belief systems: one based on an enlightened way of being; the other, largely on unconscious fear. With every thought, every word, and every action, we choose one or the other."

— **Sheila M. Kelly,** Certified Coach

"Everything is energy. We are energy personified. Love is the highest spark of energy, and when we interact with the world from our heart, we illuminate the path for others."

— **Linda Gillan**, Mentor and Advocate for Mental Health

"Financial planning is much like any other form of goal-setting. If you fail to plan today, you are by default planning to fail tomorrow. In a similar vein, oftentimes by sacrificing some of our spending power today, we can, in turn, protect and grow our standard of living in retirement for tomorrow and beyond."

— **Jason Desaulniers**, Financial Advisor, Excalibur Executive Planning Inc.

"The greatest impact on your health is you! You make the choices that will build or tear down. Learn the whys and hows to support the amazing healing capacity within."

— **Susanne Morrone**, Consultant to Aspiring Health Champions

"New beginnings and miracles await your readiness. Releasing and healing from the past allows fresh, new energies to enter. This transforms us to awaken to a more brilliant version of ourselves where magic awaits."

— **Heather Corinne Lang**, Owner, Namaste Rays

"Be the *star* of your own life. *Strive* to see what's important today and for the future; *thrive* by engaging, loving, and learning all your life; and *reconcile* by letting go of what never was or ever will be."

— **Dianne Gaudet**, Coach, Author, and Speaker

"Love is the cement that binds all existence. Fear is the sand that mixes with it to create the duality of concrete (material) existence. Your heart is the water that determines the outcome of your existence. Less heart = less water, which equates to hardness. More heart = more water, which equates to softness. Constantly pour your heart into anything and everything."

— **Mohamed Imraan Omar**, Author of
The Arabic Quran: A Journey into Consciousness

"Life doesn't truly begin until we can rest comfortably in our own skin."

— **G. Brian Benson**, Author, Actor, Musician

"Life is a journey; there are always desired moments and unfavorable moments. Just always remember, you were born crying, so die smiling."

— **Ryan J. Alsop**, Food Service,
Customer Service, and Boys and Girls Club

"You can be a victim, or you can be victorious. You cannot be both, so please choose one now."

— **Tom Justin, CEO,** Center Mass Communications, LLC

"You have opened up my heart and created a well-being."

— **Karen Brown**, Entrepreneur and Independent Contractor

"The mysteries of life are the same as the mysteries in mine. A secret."
— **Lorraine Price**, Author, Proofreader, Book and Movie Reviewer

"We all have our own story in life that has been shaped into who we are. Sometimes we are force-fed life's sandwiches, and other times, we eat our own. We manifest our actions into personal life sandwiches that we either enjoy or destroy. Open your eyes, extend your hands, and fill your hidden inner being with passion!"
— **Mark Morbeck**, Co-Owner and Motivational Speaker, Positive Sandwich Plus

"Be the game changer. Build your dreams. Breathe in your successes. Breathe away fears. You are the change."
— **Becky Wells**, Hypnotherapist, Director of Becky Wells Limited

"Communicate your message so clearly that your services, products, or programs rip off your potential client's Band-Aid, allowing you to be there to tend their wounds."
— **Darren Carrington**, CEO and Founder of Better Videos, More Clients

"To change the world, you must start with changing the conversation that goes on in your own head. Stop being so hard on yourself. You have a God-given light, and when you realize that, you begin to light up the world around you. Be someone's miracle today—that someone may be you."
— **Becky De Acetis**, Personal and Marketing Growth Consultant

"You need to think on how you reach your goals, rather than what's missing; you need to focus on what's important to you and not on what's necessary (or urgent); you need to start now, and you need to start to make actual progress toward what you want. You need to move and act now, not because you want to avoid something but because you want to achieve something!"
— **Takis Athanassiou**, e-Business/e-Learning Consultant

"The biggest change I made to create a successful company was to transition from a selfish company based on sales to a selfless company based on impact. I spend more time getting excited for others and helping them reach their dreams, and the results have been paid back 100 times."

— **Dr. Rob Garcia**, *Shift* Magazine

"Do your best each day to give another soul hope. Encourage them to believe in themselves. The greatest reward you will receive is watching them prosper."

— **Antonio D. Olivarez Jr.**

"We are all intertwined, so it's inevitable that our daily actions impact each other—whether it's just our mood in passing or what we say or do to others. As the author of *The Energy of Words*, I know how what we say, regardless of what is said, leaves a mark on our soul."

— **Michelle Arbeau**, Celebrity Numerologist, Author, Speaker, and Radio/TV Host, CEO of Authentic You Media

"We are conditioned to need validation to be successful. You won't find true success until you throw the need for validation out the window. Once you don't need validation from anyone else, you have taken the first step to creating real success for yourself!"

— **Lucas Barra**

"Don't let anyone stop you. Be unstoppable. Move whatever obstructs you out of your way and keep going faster and harder until you accomplish what you set out to do. And then, keep going."

— **Carlene Chaisson**, Realtor, Remax Nova

"Don't wait for others to give you permission to succeed; be yourself or shine your light. Give yourself permission to be your authentic self today; after all, there is only one make and model of you! True freedom is being you without anyone's permission."

— **Karie Millspaugh**, International Business and Lifestyle Coach

"Sure, the cost to maintain leadership integrity is expensive, but the cost of neglect is way more expensive."

— **Chester Goad**, Author of *Purple People Leader*

"Someday is not a day of the week."

— **Jayne Rios**, CEO, WGLA; President, WBTVN: Women's Broadcast Television Network, Founder, Spirit Fed Life

"I release what no longer serves who I am now. I embrace what best defines me."

— **Pamela Steele**, Co-Founder, Director at Brooks Medieval Faire/Author, The Cartomancer

"A 'thriver' is someone who adapts to whatever life gives them, knowing there is something positive in the end."

— **Zaheen Nanji**, Resilience Champion, Author, and Speaker

"There are two types of people in this world: those that work and those that watch them at work. I don't mind the audience."

— **Anthony Trucks**, Former NFL player, Business Coach, Author, Speaker, Life Navigator

"I would like my legacy to be that I served, that I helped when I could, and that I was kind . . . that I was a good person."

— **Skye Dyer**, Singer, Songwriter, Performer

"Resilience will always trump survival."

— **Paul Roy**

"When your self-talk is beating you down, you are in an abusive relationship with you. Stop it. Be as nice to yourself as you are to a treasured friend."

— **Genie Lee Perron**, Owner at Heal Your Life Center of Plymouth

"To find our purpose in our life, we simply have to look to the pain of our past. Darkness is the womb in which the light is born."

> — **Ricky Goodall**, Professional Lifestyle Coach

"Find a quiet place; imagine what you want. Then, let the universe lead the way. The right people and circumstances will appear. Be patient. Do not put a time limit on your dreams."

> — **Michael P. Currie**, President of Landlord by Design

"What if your subconscious mind is your Wise Protector, and when material surfaces that causes you pain, it is there to help you heal and not to bring you harm?"

> — **Rhonda Moore**, Licensed Professional Counselor and National Certified Counselor

"Attitudes are contagious. Is yours worth catching?"

> — **Coach Jim Johnson**, Coach, Bestselling Author, Speaker

"If you wish to begin living a fulfilling life, you must be able to write down and become clear on what is absolutely the most important to you. Then, trust in the actions you need to take to get there."

> — **Trevor Wilkes**, Founder, TheKnowExpert

"Change is a given; how you move through it is a choice."

> — **Tammy Braswell**, Energetic Creation Coach and Teacher, Healer, Intuitive at Create By Vibration LLC

"I am a seventy-five-year-old Alkalarian, and I walk the talk. I use an alkaline protocol that has been around over one hundred years, and it works. My passion, desire, and dream is for you to have the truth about how to live a long and healthy life and not die before your time. My goal is to die at a very young biological age at a very old chronological age."

> — **Richard Davidson**, Alkalarian

"Imagine: You are the balloon, happy thoughts the helium. Rise up and live happy!"
— **Terri Lynn**, Corporate Trainer and Development Manager
at MMCO Auto LLC, Author

"The wise person does not create positive impact through making lots of noise; by quietly acting in the spirit of service, they inspire others to do the same."
— **Coach Nick Pereira**

"Momentum—a crucial part of success. Without it, we are either stagnant, stuck in the past, or moving in a direction other than where we actually want to be going. Momentum with intention and a clear goal, that is how success is reached!"
— **Satya Chaisson**, Health and Wellness Coach

"Growing old gracefully, we mature, we become wiser, we let go, we change. We must acknowledge, we must accept, and we must learn to love who we are. Grow old and love the change."
— **Ray Chappell**, Owner, CEO, and Founder at Saving Space Yoga

"Awakening happens as we learn to observe ourselves. Enlightenment happens as we learn to love ourselves."
— **Emily Harrison**, Akashic Records Mentor

"The secret to impact is simple: create a compelling and vivid vision of where you are heading and what it will look like when you get there. Then speak that vision into existence: first in your mind, then into the hearts and minds of those who will be served and those who will help you make it a reality."
— **Michael Hudson**, Speaker, Writer, Coach, and Ideapreneur

"Art everywhere inspires me—whether it was my own art, my father's art, art I saw on walls, or even my mom's best friend, who was an amazing artist who inspired me when I was a kid. Now, and as I grew to become more knowledgeable about art, I went to the old masters to have more inspiration . . . I wanted to try to get as close as possible to reaching my peak.

— **Ami James**, Tattoo Artist, Owner of Love Hate Social Club

"The best way to create and grow a personal brand—one must adopt a message, adopt a platform and find your audience. You already have the skills and resources. Find your voice and share your message to the world."

— **Michelle Ngome,** Networking Coach, Author of *Network, Navigate, and Nurture: The Equation to Strategic Networking*

"You are greater and more powerful than you think you are."

— **Brian K. Wright**, Author and Host of *Success Profiles Radio*

"Love yourself as much as you want to be loved. Self-love is the keystone to setting healthy boundaries, making decisions, and implementing healthy habits that nurture your mind, body, and soul. When you are your best version of you, love comes to you naturally."

— **Anna Pereira,** Founder, Circles of Inspiration

"We have the ability to shape our lives as much as they shape us."

— **Joscelyn Duffy**, Transformational Storyteller, Author, Awareness/Healing Speaker, Creative Consultant/Ghostwriter

"I can design my life the way I want it or just let life happen to me. Either way, it is a choice."

— **Sharon Worsley**, Chief Inspiration Officer

"Live your life to the best of your ability. Take all of your failures and learn from them. Move forward with passion and help others from your experience. That is what life is all about." #worklifefit

— **Deborah Crowe**, Work-Life Fit Expert, Speaker, Author

"My belief is that all aspects of our being (that is to say physical, emotional, mental, and spiritual) must be in alignment and must be listened to with equal measure in order to live life with a true, felt sense of the vastness of who we truly are."

— **Moira Hutchison**, Founder at Wellness with Moira

"Life happens for you, not to you. Every event brings you a deeper relationship with your Beloved Self and your Beloved Life. This is especially true for the courageous entrepreneurial adventurer."

— **Ande Lyons**, Enthusiastic Entrepreneur,
Startup BIz Dev Coach, Happiness Instigator

"Our fears in life are often due to the illusion that life is meant to be perfect. This interferes with the natural flow of life that, if left uninterrupted, would perfectly express its ebbing flows of light and dark. This is one of the simple principles to life embedded within each of our souls that allows us to be human."

— **Dean Griffiths**, The Soul Whisperer

"If it is the truth that sets you free, is it untruths that keep you imprisoned? You are powerful when you stand naked in your truth. The world will strain its ears to hear the soft whispers from your heart. The reaction of others is simply their own reflection. You will attract your tribe and deflect those of an incongruent vibration. Be grateful for this process of natural selection."

— **Dena Churchill**, CEO and Founder of
Oxford Chiropractic Inc., International Speaker

"Time to clear out all the clutter, that which is harmful or painful. It's time to make space for all the new possibilities. Only hold on to what is most cherished and loved."

— **Beth Bracaglia**, Chief Organizing Officer/
Simplicity Architect at Simply Organized, Inspirational
Thought Leader at Beth Bracaglia's Simply Inspired

"Your dreams will lead you to the greatness—you came here to be for the world."
— **Debbi Dachinger**, Media Personality

"Everyone has struggled, or is struggling, with something—often many things at any given moment. Even the most footloose and fancy free, seemingly perfect, blissfully happy, and put-together people. The nature and extent of each struggle is as diverse as the seasons they encumber and the people who wage war against them—the suffering often done in silence at the hands of shame. Some we wear like a cloak, more visibly weighing us down, and others are inner battles, equally cumbersome, that others may know nothing about. We all face various trials and tribulations in life, but we don't always talk about them vulnerably. Perhaps if we did, people might feel a little less alone."
— **Kathy Duguay**, Owner, Legacy Junction Studios

"Get out of your way and choose love as your guiding principle. Love—accepting your soul's essential worthiness—helps you tap your intuition to claim your power, create a juicy life (and joyous afterlife), and fearlessly dig deep to discover your personal truth, free from bias. That connects you to the mystery of life, the 'why' for everyone."
— **Robyn M. Fritz**, Intuitive and Spiritual Consultant

"If I were to sum up my life with one quote, it would be, 'Be genuine and do things with integrity.' Being authentic and genuine are two things I strive to be every day in both my personal and business life. I have found that when you speak from the heart and are authentic with people, they can, in turn, naturally see your integrity. Without integrity, I believe you close yourself off from the ability to experience the abundance that is available in the world. When you open your heart up to a larger variety of life experiences and to people who can enrich those experiences, you can truly manifest a life full of amazing experiences."
— **Angela Campagnoni**, Author, *I Want to See My Papa*,
Founder and Executive Director at Atlantic Fashion Week

"Compliment people. Magnify their strengths, not their weaknesses." Unknown, as quoted by Kaye Parker.

— **Kaye Parker**, Founder, Kaye Parker Academy

"I jump feet first into unchartered waters at the start of each day. I ask myself if I'm getting closer to where I'm trying to go. At every turbulent juncture in my life's journey, I've noted that difficult waters are reinvented into fruitful estuaries. You don't cross these waters by wading in against the current. The smarter thing to do is to go with the flow and let the current carry the burden. Every good fisherman knows the life-saving skill of stepping down and across as you wade through unsettled waters. Conserve your energy, and trust that things are not going against you but rather leading you where you are meant to be. You can't become what you need to be by standing in one place."

— **Kathryn Maroun**, Executive Producer of *What a Catch*

"If you need help, ask for it, but look inside first. Sometimes we get lazy and ask others to do the work we need to step into ourselves. Look for the answer in the stillness of the question before you rush to panic for input."

— **Lana Grant**, Singer-Songwriter and Living Enthusiast

"Recognize that others may not be able to love you the way you need to be loved. They can only love you within their own capability. But it's never too late to be to yourself what you wish others had been for you. Self-care and self-nurturing isn't a selfish act; it's an act of love, and you're totally worth it!"

— **Leslie L. Sommers**, Reiki Master and Teacher

"We are all connected like beams of light to the sun, so we must be kind to others, for we're all truly one. No matter where we come from in terms of color or race, we're linked one and all to this brilliant light place."

— **Susanne Heaton**, Award-Winning Author, Empowerment Coach,, Inspirational Speaker, and Workshop Facilitator

"Big Blend is a company based on the belief that education is the most formidable weapon that can be waged against fear, ignorance, and prejudice. It is our belief that education starts at home and branches outward. Education leads to travel—and travel leads to understanding, acceptance, and appreciation of cultures and customs different to our own and, ultimately, to world peace. Our company is further based on the principle that networking, communication, and helping others to promote and market themselves leads to financial stability, thus paving the way to better education, travel, and the spirit of giving back to the community."

— **Lisa Smith** and **Nancy Reid**, Hosts of the Big Blend
Radio Show Network and the Big Blend Brand of Magazines

"Creating reality has much more to do with what is unseen and denied in the psyche than setting positive intentions. Once the shadow is illuminated, then the essence of what you truly desire can have wings. After all, the world is a mirror of everything that we are, especially that which we can't see."

— **Colette Baron Reid**, Intuitive Spiritual Teacher,
Psychic Medium, TV and Radio Host

"Stand still for a moment and notice how everything around you is quietly, vibrantly alive. It is in this presence that you'll remember your true nature."

— **Hana Holbus**, Hana's Teachings

"You are who you are for a reason. You're not supposed to be compared because there is no comparison to you. Stop wasting time doubting yourself, doubting your skill set, doubting your worth, doubting the timing, doubting if you'll make it. You've made it when you make the decision to stop questioning yourself and start taking consistent, intentional action."

— **Karen Donaldson**, Communication and
Confidence Coach, Speaker, Bestselling Author

"We are quick to take our cars in for a tune-up or get that special part for a boat. And we'll fix any problem with our house. But when it comes to our bodies, we don't go for a check-up until it's too late. Seems pretty crazy."

— **Thomas Cantley**, Founder at Mr. Ballsy

"Getting Parkinson's at age forty-five turned my world upside down but over time became the best thing that ever happened to me."

— **Peter Davison**, Founder at *Gift of the Hit: Collected Stories Books*, Advisor at Bedford Orthotics

"Creating joy in other's lives—let that be your legacy."

— **Thomas Edward Ziemann**, Spiritual Mentor and Motivational Speaker, Author, *Taming the Anger Dragon: From Pissed Off to Peaceful*

"Every day, when I awake, I am grateful to open my eyes and be able to say thank you to my Creator. It is then that I make a choice to see the beauty of my future, as I am no longer held hostage by the darkness of my past."

— **Don Kennedy**

"When making someone's day also makes your day, it's a great day!"

— **Bill Madder**, Chief Executive Officer, Association of Saskatchewan Realtors

"Passion is the soul's creative force . . . When you find your passion, it's like the sun coming out; it's pure happiness."

— **Don Jose Ruiz**, Toltec Teacher and Author

"We may not control the world, but our work of art is our own life, and even if we don't control the world, we are the co-creators. For example, we can create an impact with a single word."

— **Don Miguel Ruiz Jr.**, Toltec Teacher and Author

"The single greatest 'people skill' is a highly developed and authentic interest in the other person."

— **Bob Burg**, Coauthor of *The Go-Giver*

"Education goes far beyond what children learn in a classroom. The single most important academic skill needed today is the ability to read. Reading allows children to develop critical-thinking skills and creativity, as well as teaching them to become independent learners. Teaching children to be flexible problem-solvers with the ability to collaborate with others will go further than any knowledge learned from a book. These skills are critical to future success and can be developed through team sport. Academics and team sports go hand in hand."

— **Lorelei Burgess**, Center Director, Oxford Learning

"Making sure you get to the root cause is critical before you start to move, meditate, and eat your way to a better you. Once you know your why, you are then, and only then, able to do what you need to improve. The most important skill in any relationship is to listen. Listen to your body; it will tell you what it needs."

— **Kim Laughlin**, Health Coach

"Collaboration and implementation sparks innovation."

— **Zeb Welborn**, Owner at 19th Hole Media

"What do babies, puppies and thoughts have in common? Babies and puppies attract high vibrations. (People love them.) Your thoughts attract high/low vibrations (positive/negative). A three-step process: monitor, edit, and replace your low vibrational thoughts and create the life you want."

— **Faye Read**, Certified Self-Talk Trainer

"Life unfolds exactly the way it needs to. The most important breath you take is the one before you speak. It is the breath of consideration. Life doesn't happen to you; it happens for you."

— **Amy McNaughton**, CEO and Founder at Capable Confident Women

"Most of what I've learned in my life, I've had to learn from my mistakes, and I think that is the case for most people. The first thing I learned about show business is the only consistency is there's no consistency. The second thing was you should only hold your breath when you're underwater."

— **Mike Allan MacDonald**, Canadian Comedy Legend

"My most precious asset is my time. Don't mess with my time."

— **Emily Fisher**, #bosslady, Success Coach

"When you're a kid and you're trying to figure out who you truly are or what you're here to do. I felt like in the mid-late 80s, you were pretty much either one way or the other. Punk and rock, combined with skateboarding, that was all kind of one side, and the other side was so different, and now pretty much everything is blurred into one thing. But as far as something that kind of pulled me in and was a huge scene of this greatness that I sort of stumbled upon for whatever reason, that scene (of punk and rock music, skateboarding) was kind of everything for me back then. I really don't know how it would have gone otherwise."

— **Dan Smith**, Owner, Artist, Musician, Captured Tattoo

"As soon as you put that effort out there and you say, let me transform this tiredness—this life that you are living every day—into something that will transform somebody else, you will find your purpose."

— **Simonetta Lein**, Fashion Influencer, Huff Po, Writer, Millennial-Activist, Founder of The Wishwall Foundation

"If you don't have a dog in the fight and you are not a paid political commentator who makes money from sharing your opinion, stay silent on it (politics, religion, gender preference). You can search through years and years of my Twitter feed, and you will not be able to determine my political opinion based on my Twitter feed. I love everybody and want everybody to be able to buy my book or listen to my podcast. If you owned a coffee shop, how well would it serve your business to say, 'We only support left-handed people'? Am I going to feel comfortable coming to your coffee shop as a right-handed person, knowing right away that I'm not welcome there? It serves no purpose for your brand to comment one way or the other."

— **Bruce Van Horn**, Social Media Influencer

On what she looks for in a speaker/presentation: "At the end of the day, we all want to be entertained. You don't want to sit through a classroom-style session. You want to be able to relate, you want to be engaged, and you want to be entertained. It's those instructors that I bring back in over and over because, unfortunately, there are not a lot of those out there that deliver a certain consistency that they are going to get that feedback."

— **Nicole Burgess,** Meeting Planner,
Executive Director, SCMA Saskatchewan

"When we have made a positive difference in people's lives, that's success to me."

— **Bill Demchuk**

"Just don't give up; people give up far too easily in life. I get tired of the blame game. In general, we seem to find a lot of ways to waste time . . . Instead, perhaps we should get out there, take action, and do something big."

— **Kevin Sorbo**, Actor, Producer, Director, Speaker

"Loving what you do every day—every day waking up and being in love with what the day holds. That, to me, is success."

— **John David Mann**, *New York Times*
Bestselling Author and Entrepreneur

"Regardless of your passion, if it's being a writer, for instance, it's pretty hard to be a writer full time at the start, but if it's your passion, you will make time to get better at what you love doing. You sometimes have to be a bit crazy about your passion, as there are always ways to stoke that passion. And if you do something every day to be at least one percent better at it, you're absolutely headed in the right direction."

— **Mitch Clarke**, UFC/MMA Fighter

"If you can do what you love, then you're successful. If you're a musician and you want to, and get to, tour the world, that's success. Just the same, a guy that hasn't had a job in ten years and gets a job as a garbage man and gets to support his family and come home every night to them, that is a success. Everyone is different. Some people feel like they need to make ten million dollars a year and have everyone know their name, but for me, when I left my job in 2003 and never went back, that was my success. To be able to turn on my drum machine every day and make beats, to feed my children each morning, and to be happy with what I'm doing—that was it for me."

— **Classified**, Hip Hop Artist/Classified Music

"Women want to be treated equally . . . not identical."™

— **Judy Hoberman**, President at Selling in a Skirt

"Regardless of the age you are when you find yourself, that is when you truly start living."

— **Dawn Sinclair**, Co-Owner at Equal Essence, Owner at Revel Staging and Design

"Your awakening to, or discovery of, something miraculous is as near as the opening of your eyes."

— **Mitchell Osborn**, Psychic Medium, Soul Coach, Hypnotherapist, Animal Communicator, Tarot and Lenormand Card Reader

"Never wait for 'your' destiny to happen because you will be disappointed. You need to create it and make it happen, otherwise 'yours' will become 'theirs.'"

— **Sandra Bellamy**, Author, Social Media Trainer, Mentor, Blogger, Designer

"Here's the thing: almost everyone in North America is watching three to six hours of television a day, and if you cut that by just one hour a day, that's like adding 365 hours a year, which equals nine-and-a-half forty-hour work weeks, or two months of your life. If we take that hour a day and devote it to education and health and inner peace . . . I mean, people always ask me what's my secret to success, and I say it's that I'm always learning, and I'm always meditating.... That one hour a day can transform your life."

— **Jack Canfield**, Author, *The Success Principles*

"One thing Warren (Buffet) said that really spoke to me is about how to live your life to the fullest every day. He said that a person should ask themselves how they want to feel when they are eighty, and what they want to have accomplished, and then reverse engineer their lives—build backwards knowing where they want to arrive. That is so powerful and yet so much in contrast to how a lot of people live their lives. Unfortunately, a lot of people are dead at twenty but don't get buried until they are eighty—the walking dead, I call them. Life is so much better when you commit to doing great work and staying true to your values."

— **Robin Sharma**, Leadership Guru and Author of Eleven International Bestsellers, Including *The Monk Who Sold His Ferrari*

"Pay attention to that little voice inside your head that says there is something about this person that I don't trust, or there is something about this person that I really, really like. I'm a big believer that you go with character over anything else."

— **Chalene Johnson**, Creator of Turbo Jam and *New York Times* Bestselling Author

"The ultimate in romance is bringing flowers to your partner, and what men don't realize is that for women, every act of love scores equal in terms of oxytocin, so you could bring her thirty-six roses and you'll get a surge of oxytocin; you can bring her one rose, and you'll get the same surge of oxytocin. It's the little things make a big difference, and this oxytocin gets used up very quickly, so you need to have consistency of little things, and that creates a whole new awareness for men that they didn't have because so many men think, 'Look, I earn a living. I work hard. I provide this. Shouldn't that be enough?'"

— **John Gray**, Relationship Expert, Author of
Men Are from Mars, Women Are from Venus

"I used to let pain and sadness defeat me and reacted by doing self-destructive things. Now I use it to fuel me and for positivity. Every time something gets to me, I run and pick up a guitar. This way, negative people can't knock you down; in fact, they contribute to your success."

— **Christine Campbell**, Award-Winning Singer/Songwriter

"I'm inspired by the smaller stories, the underdogs, the real people. There are a lot of people who have their failures to attribute to their success. That's what I like to hear because that's a reality. That's what gives the average person the real hope and the real inspiration."

— **Anna Pereira**, Founder, Circles of Inspiration

"Brian Tracy . . . says that our lives are changed by the people that we meet and the books that we read and. I will go so far as to add, by the videos that we watch. I don't know many people who can honestly say I watched TED videos and my life hasn't changed. I mean TED is a great example of life-changing content that is available for free."

— **Mike Koenigs**, Serial Entrepreneur and
Bestselling Author of *Chief Disruptasaurus*

"So many people focus on what they can get from their customers rather than what they can give . . . Money is simply an echo of value. It's the thunder to value's lightning. The value must come first, and the money you receive is simply the very natural result of the value you provide for that customer."

— **Bob Burg**, Speaker and Bestselling Author of *The Go-Giver*

"Being involved in a book launch, given today's technology, was truly quite overwhelming, but here is the way I looked at it. I could have either allowed myself to stay overwhelmed and to develop a pessimistic attitude—and some people might have just given up, maybe. Instead, I looked at it as a challenge and an opportunity that could only end up being positive and one that could allow me to grow beyond what may have otherwise been possible, and by doing that, even though at first it was quite daunting to me, as I moved along and didn't allow myself to get defeated, it actually started to become easier, and comfortable even."

— **Dr. Alan Simberg**, International Bestselling Author

"The first time I spoke in public, Corey, I was terrified. I didn't know that public speaking was the number one fear, but at the same time, I think that is when I was coming out of my shell and realizing more about what my life's purpose was and how participating in Toastmasters (to gain comfort in public speaking) was going to help me to move forward and carry my message to the people who needed to hear it."

— **Regina Rowley**, International Bestselling Author

"If you're the smartest person in the room, you have to get out of that room."
— **Tony Gambone**, Founder of the Tough Talk Radio Network

"I think it's vitality important for all entrepreneurs, regardless of the size of their entity, to constantly learn what other entrepreneurs are doing, to be constantly masterminding from other entrepreneurs, seeing what they are doing, what the downsides are, and what's really working for them, so that all of us that are living on an island, as entrepreneurs, get to see what others like us are doing so we can learn and improve."

— **Chris Stafford**, CEO and Founder of Massive Abundance

"You can accomplish more if you give your mind a break through practices like yoga and meditation."

— **Angela Bryden**, Yogi

"The three things I would tell my younger self? First, worry less. Life is short, and if I desire to create positive change and lead an adventurous, loving, and happy life, I need to take risks and be free of not only others' negativity but, in particular, my own. Secondly, be here now. Live fully, live in the moment, listen carefully, and engage in my life and in the lives of those who surround me. Lastly, take 'me' time, as doing the things you love is not time wasted."

— **Emilie Chiasson**, Volunteer

"It's not just enough for someone to say no to the things that are bad for them; they also need something to say yes to. When you say yes to something, something you're passionate about, something you nerd out about, something that you love that gives you a sort of natural high, you will absolutely protect yourself from stuff that would sabotage it or attack it. You refuse to sacrifice the great things you're doing for almost anything. That's the power of finding your passion."

— **Josh Shipp**, Youth Speaker and Teen Expert

"The people I see who have great success in today's ever-changing market are the ones who take massive action, are consistent, and they don't give up. There is more to it than that, but that is the foundation, the starting point, if you will. Without those things, nothing really happens."

— **John Tighe**, Host of the Top-Rated *Publish Position Profit* Podcast and Amazon Launch Expert

"As part of my coaching to help someone with gratitude, I tell them to pick someone in their life, and for a week make that person's dreams come true. What that can mean is if they want to go somewhere, fully support them, or if they have an idea, fully support it, and you will be surprised at the results. You'll be happier, they'll be happier, and the things you are supporting may lead to bigger and better things."

— **Gary Ware**, Life Coach and Host of *Breakthrough Cocktail* Show

"One of the biggest things I learned from Robert Kiyosaki teachings was, 'Work to learn, not to earn.'"

— **Tyler Basu,** Host of the *Chatting with Champions* Podcast

"Super-achievers and high achievers are mostly who is suffering with disorders like anxiety because the personality types that lead to these disorders are the perfectionists and the very driven people."

— **Kevin Davis**

"We're truly in balance when we're living a proactive life, rather than a reactive life. When we're living a proactive life, we have more energy, things flow more smoothly, and we're better able to be our true selves. For me, and I think it's for most, we're also able to better hear our intuition."

— **Brian B. Benson,** Author, Actor, Musician

"When people just do these formulaic affirmations, however many times a day, to try to get their energy up—which is fine because none of us want to live as victims—they sometimes forget it also takes risk-taking, sometimes failure, getting out of the comfort zone, and especially taking action to make it all come together. We truly have a gift to give, and there are a lot of hungry people out there not getting served by a person like you, and there is a big world waiting for your gift, so action is just as important as those formulaic affirmations."

— **Rebekah Carpenter,** Speaker, Performing Artist, Leadership and Organizational Development Trainer

"I can't think of anything that has ever worked out for me where I haven't messed up ten times before I got it right, but I know I'll eventually get it completely. Making mistakes and failing is truly a key part of the learning process. You're not supposed to get it right every single time . . . All I know is every single time you make a mistake and fall down, a new door opens and you learn better how to tackle something the next time. The end result is you know how to fall down better in the future, and your success—once you get it figured out—is more sustainable success in the long run."

— **Lisa Smith** and **Nancy Reid**, Hosts of the Big Blend Radio Show Network and the Big Blend Brand of Magazines

"Love the people you have. Live your life fully. Be who you are and make the relationships you have with your loved ones, and the people in your life, the most important thing. That's what you're here for."

— **Carmel Joy Baird**, Television Personality from *Mom's a Medium*

"I'm always talking to our players about the fact that if we're going to be exceptional this year, we have to be great in the things we can control. That's why we really focus on our work ethic and our attitude, because those are things we can control."

— **Jim Johnson**, Coach, Bestselling Author, Speaker

"Our approach is that we tend to bite off more than what we can chew and then we chew like hell. We have no problem getting in there doing the work, but what we were missing at the time is that there are two different sides of the business. There is the action/conscious side (marketing, selling, and service) and then there is the spiritual side (visualization, goal-setting, creating your vision board) where you're creating events to have happen for you. You need to be focused on both."

— **Natalie Ledwell**, Co-creator of the Mind Movies Brand and Host of T*he Inspiration Show*

"In my opinion, passion is all about the heart. But our mind and heart need the same fuels to co-operate with each other. I actually feel anxiety comes from too much mind and not enough heart."

— **Janet Harrison**, Reiki Master

"As we become fit and active, we naturally tend to eat better, sleep better, handle stress better, and our decision-making improves."

— **John Stanton**, Founder of the Running Room, Bestselling Author

"We have one shot at this lifetime, and we have a unique array of individual talents and gifts. And it's crucial to tap into what lights you up, puts the fire in your belly, and gets you up excited each day. Whether it's a hobby or what you do for your career, it's crucial to find it. Just don't die with that passion inside you."

— **Mari Smith**, Facebook and Social Media Expert

"If you want to be, do. I was literally horrible when I started as an interviewer, but I wanted to be a broadcasting host; I wanted to have a good broadcasting voice; I wanted to gain good interview skills, and the only way for me to get there was to actually do it. My first step was just getting on a microphone, and everything developed from that. If I hadn't taken action, nothing would have happened. So, what I want to leave people with is simply that: if you want to be, do."

— **John Lee Dumas**, Creator of the Popular *Entrepreneur on Fire* Podcast, Author, Founder of Podcaster's Paradise and WebinarOnFire Communities

"What I would tell my younger self? Know yourself, and stay awake. Keep asking yourself every day of your life, 'Is this the real path for me?' And keep changing course to get to where you want to go. Don't stop learning; don't stop growing; don't stop setting goals; and don't stop asking, 'Is this how I want to be as a person?' I think if you keep doing that year after year, you wind up being like a great bottle of wine—thirty or forty years later, you're better and are more complex than when you began. If you don't do that, you wind up thirty or forty years later realizing you're like a bad bottle of wine; you've now gone sour in the bottle and turned to vinegar."

— **Dr. John Izzo**, Author, *The Five Secrets You Must Discover before You Die*

"I would say my earnings are a byproduct of how helpful I am to—and how good I am at serving—my audience. That is my passion, serving audiences of all types, and the more I help people, the better my life has become."

— **Pat Flynn**, Creator of *Smart Passive Income*

"I'm a big believer that there is a lot of opportunity to help a smaller group of people get together and achieve their goals. It's amazing how much of our calories are being spent doing only the big things, and it seems we're using up a lot of our time running around in circles, and I feel a better methodology might be to find a small group of people that we can accept, get to know, and understand. And then we can work better with that group."

— **Chris Brogan**, Speaker and CEO of Owner Media Group

"The real growth and real progress happens when things are hard, when we're going after things that make us so afraid. It's at those times that having someone in your corner is so important. Even if you just have a coach for a specific time in your life, a time when you know you're on the cusp of something really big, for instance—and you'll always know it's that time by how scared you are. In fact, your inner critic always seems to come out when you're on the verge of something really big. So, back to my point, even if you just have a coach during that time and take notes like mad, you'll be further ahead than if you never have a coach whatsoever."

— **Andrea Owen**, Founder of Your Kick Ass Life
and the Kick Ass Life Coach

"There is a lot of work that goes into it. I think a lot of people look at it and think it's just a twelve week competition prep, but it's way more than that. You really need to be committed, prepared, and focused. If you're not prepared, it can affect all aspects of your life, whether it be relationships, family. You really need to be sure that you're surrounded by the right people if you want to get into this seriously because not everybody understands why you'd want to step onto the stage in the tiniest bikini in your entire life and diet for so many weeks to fit into that bikini. I think the big challenge is making sure you have a good support group with you."

— **Melissa White**, Fitness and Bikini Model

"The high achievers know how to remain all in and focused when it comes to the person in front of them and the task they are currently working on."

— **Mike Lipkin**, Speaker and Bestselling Author

"It pays to be innovative. If you are innovative, you can expect to fail more often than you succeed, but if you think about it on a graph, everybody crowds around in one spot where the successful things are, and if you want to take a chance and go higher on the graph on the X-Y scale, and if it hits, you're the only one there. You can have tremendous success that way. Innovation breeds success."

— **Dave Carroll**, Speaker, Musician, Author, and Creator of the United Breaks Guitars Brand

"Social media is a great thing because it shows us how small the world really is, and that six degrees of separation is really two . . . Every tweet's an audition in which people are watching. That's why I've come up with the four *Es* of essential tweeting . . . First, your tweet should be entertaining. It should be educational. It should enhance the lives of your audience, and it should be able to create engagements."

— **Gary Loper,** Twitter Specialist

"There is a major difference between talking about what your products and services do versus talking about what your products mean, and there is a difference between communicating with the language of information and the language of persuasion."

— **Gair Maxwell**, Branding Expert and Speaker

"Not all of us know early what our passions are, but I feel the journey of searching for it and finding it is, to me, as important as discovering what it is or they are."

— **Justin Hines**, Singer/Songwriter and Speaker

"The internet and technology has changed things remarkably, to where whole industries are becoming obsolete. We are now in a very extreme period of commoditization, and the only real safety that you actually have is in having these very, very powerful client/customer relationships where you are unusually well-informed about the future of the client/customer, but not only that, they include you in that thinking because they do their best thinking when they are with you."

— **Dan Sullivan**, Strategic Coach

"This is an exciting time! From the fields of neuroscience and neurobiology, we are learning that with a very particular set of simple tools, we can go from the most troubling of problems to its solution in sixty seconds flat."

— **Dr. Reggie Melrose**, Author and Speaker

"The distance between excellence and mediocrity is the distance between common knowledge and consistent application."

— **Mark Sanborn**, Speaker and Author of the
International Bestselling Book *The Fred Factor*

"Somehow, my need to communicate helped me overcome my fear of communicating."

— **Silken Laumann**, Olympic Athlete, Medalist

"If I was speaking to my younger self, I would say that one of the most important things in life and business is to ask the right questions. The questions that move you closer to what you want and further away from what you don't want . . . On my definition of success? I feel if you can feel proud of yourself, proud of the work you're doing, proud of your family, and proud of your business, that is success to me."

— **Steve Martile**, Online Marketing Expert,
Blogger, Founder of Blogging for Coaches

"On my whiteboard, I have something I wrote out that says that my goal, the Ziglar goal, is to be a burning torch lighting other torches. The idea behind that is it's one thing to teach somebody and get them excited, but significance comes when you're able to give somebody some truth and their fire gets lit and they go out and light other people's fires."

— **Tom Ziglar**, President of Ziglar Inc., Speaker, and Proud Son of the Late Zig Ziglar

"I've been blessed to read a lot. Once I learned to read, which was at age eighteen, I devoured books. I've read 29,503 books now, that I've documented. So, I constantly read, and I've studied the Nobel Prize winners, the greatest philosophers, the greatest religious leaders, the most accomplished entrepreneurs, the greatest in finances, and I try to empower myself by studying and standing on the shoulders of giants in all areas."

— **Dr. John Demartini**, Speaker and Founder of the Demartini Institute

"Life is never a straight line; it's always up and down. As you go forward in your life, sometimes you feel frustrated and challenged, and you're always looking for hope and inspiration. For me, inspiration always starts close to home with family and friends, but I also have role models whom I continue to look up to— people like Terry Fox, who was a good buddy. He was, and still is, an incredible inspiration to me. He encouraged me to reach for my dreams—no matter how challenging they may have seemed—and to work harder during difficult times. I also find inspiration when I meet someone new who has accomplished something incredible or someone who has overcome adversity or come at life with a great attitude. I can even feel the inspiration from them breathe life into me. What I have learned is that all of us have that opportunity to be inspired if we're open to it."

— **Rick Hansen**, The "Man in Motion," Author, Speaker

"When someone tells me my product costs too much, I say, 'Hot dog, they are going to own it because they have a desire, but want it for less.' Now, my goal as a pro is to realize they want the product, and I as a pro, in my presentation skill, I have to do something through the art of my presentation to help them rationalize the investment."

— **Tom Hopkins**, Author of *How to Master the Art of Selling* (Bestselling Sales Book in History)

"A lot of the work I do is about how you can be one of a kind instead of one of many because the world doesn't need another coach, another speaker, another coffee shop, another author. It does need and want someone or something who is the first of their kind, somebody who is doing something in a way that hasn't been seen before, and somebody who is introducing something fresh."

— **Sam Horn**, The Intrigue Brand, Author of *POP!* and *Tongue Fu*- Website

"I often talk about helping business leaders through the maze. There are left and right turns that you should just not make, and there are other turns that you have to make to get to the finish line. The goal of people like myself in writing is to help people avoid making every mistake themselves."

— **Dr. Joseph Michelli**, The Michelli Experience, Author of *The Starbucks Experience*

"People ask me all of the time, 'What is organic food?' and my answer is always the same. I tell them that organic food is what we've been eating and growing since the beginning of time . . . and the other food is so altered, we had to rename it organic food to define the difference."

— **Lil MacPherson**, Founder of the Wooden Monkey

"You're going to get told what you can and can't do a lot in your life, but it's what you end up believing that ultimately ends up coming true."

— **Sean Stephenson**, Motivational Speaker and Bestselling Author

"How many times have people heard stories of going to an open mic in somewhere like LA and seeing Jay Leno there practicing his stuff, or some big-name comic, because they know that nothing is better than a real live audience to rehearse your stuff. A mirror doesn't cut it; your spouse doesn't cut it; your kids really don't cut it."

— **Michel Neray**, Speaker and Founder of MoMondays

"When you act out of desperation, you cut yourself off from your passion and that which you were meant to do. If you follow your passion and make it work for you, the finances soon follow. My grandfather taught me a great lesson because I've also had to take jobs that I didn't want to do so that I could put food on the table, but he said work that job as if you are following your passion, and it then created the access for me to go into what I really wanted to do."

— **Rain Pryor**, Actress, Comedienne, Playwright

"The primary common trait of super-achievers—and this is across the board, there are no exceptions, that I know of, and I have spoken with thousands of people. I've worked with 6,500 people one-on-one, and I've spoken on stages with some of the most amazing people on the planet—and every single one of those people that are really and truly successful has at least one coach, somebody to work with, and somebody to walk with hand in hand and side by side, someone who's been there, and someone who can help you get through some of those rough spots."

— **Shawn Shewchuk**, Speaker and Author

"With trust, when it comes to social media, there really is no difference between online and face to face . . . On social media, you still have to make promises and keep them; you've got to build your reputation; you have to do what you say you're going to do, and you have to attribute the sources for the data that you put out there. The good news is, you can build your brand even faster because once you do get a reputation on social media, you can amplify your reputation to the good end . . . but the reverse is also true."

— **Greg Link**, Co-founder of the Covey Leadership Center

"A German philosopher once said, simplicity is the ultimate sophistication, and I really like that quote, and I share that with my clients and audiences. Like you said, on the surface, things look pretty easy, but it's hard work to stick to your principles, to manage by your values and be true to your values—especially in today's economic climate."

— **Bill Capodagli**, Capodagli Jackson Consulting, the Disney Way Brand

"How do you sell something that no one wants? Like selling beds in a nursing home? The simple answer is through hearing conversations. The conversations I have had with seniors and their loved ones have taught me how to hear what is being said or not being said. The clues are there; you just have to hear the conversation being shared with you."

— **Tami Neumann**, Founder of the Conversations in Care Brand

"It's important to understand that if you're not moving toward excellence, you're moving away from it, and it works the same with the FISH philosophy in the (*FISH!*) book, which is choose your attitude, be playful, be present with people, and make their day. You put all those things together, and you're always going to be working toward excellence."

— **Harry Paul**, Coauthor of *FISH!* and
author of *Who Kidnapped Excellence?*

"We have taken away the ability to fail from people. We call it self-esteem. In my opinion, we've actually got things backwards. When you grow up without arms, and you're learning to use your feet—granted, it was the '60s in my case—your failure becomes part of your default mechanism every single day. My mother taught me a very valuable lesson when I was growing up, learning to use my feet, because using your feet for everything isn't easy, but using your feet is like a metaphor for anything else in society—if everything was easy, where would be the challenge, and if we have no challenge, what's the point? I often hear from teenagers that life is not fair. My answer is, right. Now, where is the discussion from there? Because life's not fair, but it can be incredible . . . and when you learn how to succeed because you have failed a few times, that is a great lesson that we can take into everything in our world."

— **Alvin Law**, Motivational Speaker

"Our only obstacle is often our own mind. Things can come up in our own mind, like, 'You don't have an event-planning degree,' or 'You don't have a production degree. What am I going to say to these people?' But if you try, and let the chips fall where they may, you'll be amazed by what can happen. You just have to speak your truth, show up, and ask for what you want. We certainly don't do that enough."

— **Anne Berube**, Life Coach and Founder of Autopoetic Ideas

"If you choose to have partners in any aspect of your life, it is important to have the right ones. In our case, each partner has unique strengths and experience, which have helped make us a smarter, better organization. We have different viewpoints but a common goal and vision. I am certain that if it hadn't been for our partnership, PropertyGuys.com would not be what it is today."

— **Ken Leblanc**, PropertyGuys.com

"My goal is to help you take charge of your own health and kick disease to the curb. My approach is to teach, consult, and coach you into effective action."

— **Gloria Askew**, Author of *Eat to Save Your Life*

"If a person as a manager can be able to have a solid team in place, then there is no limit to what they can do and what they can reach in their career."

— **David Long**, Speaker, Life Coach, Author

"If we truly focus on patient care, what's best for the patient, we'll want to have a team of people working with our patients to keep their temple healthy. You need a team of people. Just like you need a team of people to build and maintain a house (you need a plumber, an electrician, a painter) you need a team of people working together—somebody for acute care, somebody for wellness care—to maintain your body to be healthy and vital for the longest period of time."

— **Dena Churchill**, Speaker, Author, Chiropractor

"You are the company you keep. So if you're hanging out with a bunch of rock climbers and that's your circle of friends, you're probably going to be a rock climber. If you're sitting around with a bunch of couch potatoes, you're probably going to sit on the couch. So accountability comes with who you are spending a lot of your time with. If you don't have any athletic friends, if you don't have an athletic family, if you don't have people that are interested in that, then you've got to go find them—whether they be online, in your neighborhood, at your local school, at work, or whatever they are out there, and you just have to be proactive when it comes to finding them. They are not going to come knocking on your door, so you have to go knocking on their door."

— **Tony Horton**, Creator of P90x

"Focusing on helping people, not myself, has been the largest contributor to my success in generating over twenty-five million dollars online since 2007, working from home, with no office and no employees."

— **Chris Luck**, Serial Entrepreneur, Coach

"There are sides to this equation, just like there are two sides to working out. You have to intend and be committed, and you actually have to hit the floor and do the push-ups. So, if you want to design your life, you have to build a design you believe in and are passionate about, and then you have to start yesterday and take action in the direction you have so gleefully posted on your vision board and move with every intuition and thought in that direction. Otherwise, you're no different than all the dreamers that sat and wished for stuff. Amen!"

— **Kellan Fluckiger**, Coach, Speaker

"Don't worry about finding your passion in life. Just look for something that you feel you will enjoy… By finding the thing that you enjoy and then becoming as good as you can be at it, then you are ahead of 90 percent of the people on earth. Throw in an obsession with research to become even better, and not only will you be in the top two percent, but also you have turned your like into a passion. That's how it's done."

— **David Ralph**, Host and Creator of the *Join Up Dots* Podcast

"Success is like sausage; you'd be surprised what goes into it." (In other words, there are a lot of decidedly unglamorous aspects to making a business work.)

— **Tim Fargo**, Author of *Alphabet Success*

"Go where you are celebrated, not where you are tolerated, and you will always be appreciated."

— **Dr. Frederick Jones**, Speaker

"In terms of choosing your own attitude, I believe you can start your day over anytime. If you wake up and stub your toe, it could ruin your whole day if you let it. I mean, watching somebody throw their dog up in the air and catch it three times getting more views than mine on YouTube could, of course, cause me to be bitter, but why would I want to do that when I could instead say this is what people are watching, so I have to take responsibility for the excitement of my own presentation and proceed accordingly. It's all a matter of choice."

— **Mark Goffeney**, Singer/Songwriter, Speaker

"There is time to do everything God created you to do; there is not time to do everything. There is not time to do everything good. There's not time to do everything everyone else wants you to do. And, there's not even time to do everything you want to do. But, if God is God, then there *is* time to do everything he created you to do."

— **Marnie Swedberg**, Author, Speaker, Media Guest

"Whatever goal you have in mind, it's about making decisions along the way that you can look back on and have no regrets. If I had skipped a workout day because I needed to recover and let my body heal, that's a decision I would never regret. If I took a day off, though, just because I didn't feel like working out that day, and I didn't achieve my goal, and there was a chance it could have been because of that skipped day, that would have haunted me. So, live in a way that you'll have no regrets."

— **Heather Moyse**, Two-Time Olympic Gold Medalist

"In terms of success in life, I've learned that if I get nothing more out of life than to learn something new every day, then, to me, I've been successful, or at least I've had fulfillment in my life. For me, every day I feel like I'm creating a painting. Some days, it's a great painting; some days, not so much. At least I'm still painting."

— **Jeff Doyle**, Founder of SmileDog Reception

"When I think about jumping into business in spite of all the obstacles facing me at the time, I feel it's summed up best by what British producer Mark Burnett has said: 'There's nothing like biting off more than you can chew, and then chewing anyway.' I find I'm constantly chewing like heck, and I wouldn't have it any other way."

— **Blaise Curry**, President of Atlantic Marketing with Apeele

"The only real wealth that has value is the amount in which we serve those who are in need. Money, fame, power—all these will fade away. Love that is spread through service is eternal."

— **Luke McClure**, Founder of Married Life Coaching, Co-Founder of the *Exchange* Podcast Community, Podcaster

"I feel like the trenches of entrepreneurship are beautifully tumultuous: it's excruciating and exhilarating at the same time. But it's definitely not for the faint of heart. Sometimes, you can't help but feel like it just may be the death of you, but there is no alternative. It's all about becoming the person you feel you were meant to become. Nothing beats the feeling of those 'aha' moments when it all comes together."

— **Kathy Duguay**, Founder of the Legacy Junction, Photographer

"When I first started coaching fifty-four years ago, if I had known how little I knew, I probably would have been discouraged and quit. Now, all these years later, I realize how much I still have to learn, so I keep trying to learn more."

— **Allan Andrews**, Founder of Andrew's Hockey Growth

"A lot of the high-achieving people that I've come into contact with, I've noticed they are very accommodating; they are very engaged in the person they are speaking with, and they have great people skills. Now, of course, not every high achiever has great people skills or is genuine, but I feel a lot of them are. Sidney (Crosby) is a great example; he's someone who has great values and very good people skills. I feel that even though not everyone who has achieved at the highest level is a nice guy, a common trait of high achievers is genuine people skills."

— **Doug Shepherd**, Elite Skating Coach,
Executive Director of Andrew's Hockey Growth

"In sport, the fundamental purpose isn't necessarily financial gain. Sport puts you in situations where you win and lose, where you work hard and you try to be your best at all times. Sometimes things don't work out, but you gain from that as well—you gain emotionally while developing some internal strengths. You're also able to learn about setting goals and how best to strive to achieve them. The lessons of sport are huge."

— **Wally Kozak**, Olympic Hockey Coach

"We rarely forget to feed our body, but sadly, we often forget to feed our mind."

— **Corey Poirier**, International Bestselling Author, TEDx Speaker,
Host of the *Conversations With PASSION!* Radio Show

"I find with so many people their health is holding them back, and it's not because they are not trying; it's just that they are following the wrong set of rules. They are getting hit with the misinformation out there that is so rampant in our industry. So, that's my crusade, to show people that. I believe if people knew better, then they would do better, and it's so easy to turn your health around and to be healthy. It's actually so much easier than a lot of the experts would have to you believe, and when you do that, then you can really step out and do the things you were meant to do in your life and not have things like your energy, your weight, or pain hold you back."

— **JJ Virgin**, Celebrity Nutritionist and Fitness
Expert, *New York Times* Bestselling Author

"When I spoke with people, yes, mentorship did come up often, and a lot of people said they had mentors, and the process of mentorship helped them—just not as many as the eight common traits. Still, what may surprise you is that I couldn't find a case where people said that mentors pushed them to succeed, and yet, there were many cases where people said that tormentors had pushed them to succeed—tormentors meaning people who said the highly successful leaders and achievers of today couldn't do what they ultimately end up doing. Those tormentors were bigger driving forces than mentors they worked with. Just something I found interesting as it wasn't necessarily what I expected."

— **Richard St. John**, Author of *8 to Be Great*, TED speaker

"I see a lot of entrepreneurs struggle with their worth, and in many cases, give away their time, knowledge, and talents because they don't believe, deeply enough, that what they have to offer is something that people will pay for. If you don't value your time, neither will others. Stop giving away your time and talents and start charging for it."

— **Kim Garst**, Branding Expert

"When you choose to *not* live in mediocrity, you shake up everybody else's world. The Defining Difference occurs when you shake up your life. Take a chance. Live on purpose. Take deliberate risk for the sake of growth. It will fuel your soul."

— **Cindy Ertman**

"You can't successfully navigate through the obstacles in front of you if you're constantly looking behind you."

— **Marcia Olsen**, Diet, Fitness, and Lifestyle Coach

"I'll be out for a jog, and I'll be thinking about how my leg is hurting, and I'll look to the left and see somebody who is having a more difficult time; perhaps they are in a wheelchair and not jogging at all. It's all about perspective, and I think that when you open your eyes to those lessons, and to the universe, it makes the journey so much easier."

— **Candace Carnahan**, Motivational Speaker

"Balance is critical to every life. God knows we need capacities for different kinds of relationships that can contribute to our overall well-being and satisfaction in life. I believe goal-setting in the form of keeping a written schedule of appointments and activities can help anyone maintain balance in their life. When we are mentally prepared to change gears, we are more inclined to be fully engaged and dedicated to the activity at hand."

— **Zig Ziglar**, Bestselling Author, Motivational Speaker

"My approach to life is that I get up every day, and I don't know what the future holds each day. The only thing I know for sure is that I want to make a difference in this world and grow as a person each day. That's perhaps why every career or project I have been involved with has always been tied to giving back to the community and a charity. I really feel it's our responsibility to grow while we give back and strive to make a difference."

— **Nikki Jafari**, Founder of International Business Tradeshow

"When you are focused and creating relevancy with something powerful, you may just find that your niche is actually a mass."

— **Mitch Joel**, President of Mirum and Author
of *Six Pixels of Separation* and *CTRL ALT Delete*

"One of the greatest gifts you can give yourself in today's high-wants, easy-credit, disposable society is to learn to live without a dependency on credit and to really value the important things in life. There is a lot of truth to the saying, 'Money cannot buy (real) happiness.' Live simply. Love freely. And spend consciously."

— **Mary Ann Marriott**, Trustee in Bankruptcy (aka Dr. Debt)

"Two words I don't like to abbreviate: Pls and Thx."

— **Matt Whitman**, HRM Councilor

"Success is never without sacrifice. The farmer gets up before dawn to tend his crops. The Olympian trades social outings for yet another practice. The entrepreneur puts all her savings into the startup. By postponing pleasure, we reap the future reward of success."

— **Michelle Porter**, Founder of Souls Harbor Rescue Mission,
Regina, Saskatchewan, and Halifax, Nova Scotia

"Stop waiting around to be discovered. Discover yourself instead!"

— **Jade Simmons**, Rock-Star Concert Pianist,
Powerhouse Speaker, and Emergence Expert

"A life full of excuses is like opting out of the life you want for yourself."

— **Joel Boggess**, Speaker

"The joy in the journey comes from the sharing, for purpose-filled paths are not meant to be travelled alone."

— **Michelle Colon-Johnson**, Founder, 2 Dream Productions

"To achieve more in life and relationships, you must first let go of the endless pursuit of balance, which you will find is unattainable and immeasurable and ends only with frustration and failure. Focus instead on intentionally managing your days so that you spend more time doing meaningful activities with people you love and protecting that time from less important activities, and you will find greater fulfilment than any misguided search for 'balance' will ever yield."

— **Nick Pavlidis**, Author of *Confessions of a Terrible
Husband: Lessons Learned from a Lumpy Couch*

"Follow your heart wherever it leads. No one should be working in a job that they hate. No one should be stuck in a relationship that they don't want to be in. Own your impact and make conscious choices. If you always lead with love and if you always go with whatever your vision is—as long as it's helping, healing, or serving other people using your unique gifts and your special talents—you'll find fulfillment in life."

— **davidji**, Stress-Management Expert,
Corporate Trainer, and Meditation Teacher

"I have lost, and I have won. Sometimes when I won, I actually lost, and sometimes when I lost, I actually won. If you win but did things with the wrong intentions, then you lost. If you do things for the right reasons and lose, you actually feel like a winner!"

— **Christine McAleer**, Prince Edward Island Realtor

"The wonderfully surprising moment when your story and mine intersect— when you recognize me in you and I recognize you in me, especially when we don't expect to—well, that's the moment the world is moved. As leaders and speakers, our job is to find and share those stories."

— **Sally Koering Zimney**, Creative Consultant, Host of *This Moved Me* Podcast

"There's never been a better time to be yourself and build a life that celebrates that. Everyone has something to offer, and no matter how small your contribution feels, remember that your second nature is someone else's struggle. Success is no longer determined by how well you fit in, but is rather defined by how well you stand out. Listen more, support others' ambitions, and do the unexpected. Never forget that your *weird* is someone else's *wonderful*."

— **Craig Carpenter**, Entrepreneur and Founder of RELAY

"Progress over perfection."

— **Emily Lynn Fisher**, Blogger and Coach

"The value of your true self is displayed in your ability to be authentic in the face of judgement. It is masked by the effort to please and assimilate to those around you. Go forward with courage. Be only you."

— **Taylor MacGillivary**, Yogi and Podcaster

"Success is not measured by commas in your bank account or by the initials after your name. It is manifested by a daily commitment to show those around you their inherent worth in such a way that they feel inspired to live up to it."

— **Bryce Prescott**, Host and Creator, *Rules of Success* Podcast

"We must remember that everything we need, everything we already are, is inside us. Otherwise, we are forever giving away and delaying our path home to self. We know this is the great truth passed to us from every major religion and study, yet we complicate it and burden it with processes and rituals, comparisons and teachers. Sit still. It is all right here."

— **Lisa Marie**, Pioneer in TV and Conceptual Redefining

"It's easy to have an out-of-body experience; you have it every night. But can you handle the in-body experience?"

— **Betsy Chasse**, Author, Blogger, Speaker, Screenwriter, and Consultant

"A successful entrepreneur knows there's a good chance of failure, whereas the unsuccessful one knows there's a good chance of success. Knowing failure is where the most wisdom is gained, success comes faster."

— **Paul Colaianni**, Host of *The Overwhelmed Brain*,
Author of *How to Deal with Irrational People*

"Stop focusing on the outcome; instead, engage in the process."

— **Dekera Greene Rodriguez**, Owner, Grinding Out

"I'm a storyteller. We all are. We have different stories to tell and different reasons to tell them and different platforms to tell them from, but we are all storytellers . . . and every one of us will have a different way to share our story. If we didn't, the world wouldn't have a need for all of us."

— **Dachia Arritola**, Speaker and Storyteller

"A lot of people get bogged down or don't go for it because they think they don't have the talent or skills. Despite common beliefs, natural talent doesn't exist when you peel back the layers and dig deeper. (Mozart wasn't a prodigy, for instance.) You can become a master simply by investing the time mastering what you have a passion for. Relentless striving for excellence will make you excellent, no matter your circumstances."

— **Scott Alan Turner**, Personal Finance Expert and Serial Entrepreneur

"Clarity is to realize that our unique combination of experiences and knowledge is the secret sauce to deliver true value to those around us. To succeed, we don't have to invent the next gadget or bungee jump from the tallest building. Success comes from clarity about what we stand for and where we're headed. And once we reach clarity, we need to cherish every second we'll spend sharing our unique gifts with the world. That's where the fun lies: in the discovery, the growth, and the connections we'll make along the way."

— **Cloris Kylie**, Performance Coach and Branding Expert

"By improving our happiness, we'll become more successful. If we practice gratitude, kindness, and creativity, we'll get lives of meaning and fulfillment. Furthermore, we can model these behaviors for our kids to guide them toward the best possible future."

— **Mike Ferry**, Author of *Teaching Happiness and Innovation*

"Be the change you want to be. Design the life you want to experience."

— **Tiffany Mason**, Founder, Mason Coaching & Consulting

"You never know who you will meet or what it will lead to."

— **Michelle Ngome**, Networking Coach, Author of *Network, Navigate & Nurture: The Equation to Strategic Networking*

"The falls in your life will not hurt you until you start blaming them on others. You are responsible for everything in your life and everything that isn't. Get back up, take responsibility, and create the life you want."

— **Robin Marvel**, Author and Speaker

"Design a life of possibility rather than limitation, a life of choice not chance!"

— **Dr. Karen Jacobson**, High-Performance Strategist, Speaker, and Bestselling Author

"For me, social media is a marketing platform, and I have this idea that I can use social media as a platform if I earn that right by providing value to my followers. My idea of providing value to my followers is to constantly provide great content, whether I create it or curate it. The result is, every once in a while I can hit them [my followers] with a promotion."

— **Guy Kawasaki**, Evangelist, Author, and Speaker

"When we start to acknowledge, accept, and appreciate all the good and bad aspects of ourselves, it is then we find inner peace and truly start to live our lives authentically."

— **Di Riseborough**, Intuitive Life Strategist

"You are a beautiful, luminous soul. Celebrate yourself every day. Shine your radiant light."

— **Josefina Navarro**, Transformation Consultant, Women Sublime

"When you find the courage to forgive, you will regain the power to love."

— **Patricia Love**, Founder, Life's Cheerleader

"Tell your loved ones how much they mean to you now. Forgive those who have hurt you. Ask forgiveness from them whom you feel you may have hurt. And don't forget to treat yourself with love and respect—because you are just as important as everyone else."

— **Karen Noé**, Psychic Medium, Spiritual Counselor, and Energy Healer

"What is abundance? Devote some quality time with your inner kingdom. You will get the answer."

— **Yatin Khulbe**, Blogger

"Be open and honest with yourself when seeking answers within. These answers hold the keys to the locks that bind you."

— **Bhavya Gaur**, KindredSoulz

"Be a warrior strong and true; trust in the journey that was made just for you."

— **Kim Bayne**, Director, Live Life Positively with Kim Bayne

"Don't wait for the perfect time. Life can be wonderful within the imperfections."

— **Brenda Freeman**, Mind Recipes

"Living ecstatically is to live in alignment with your soul's calling. It is to listen to that voice whispering deep within your heart and to follow it toward your dreams. It is to be authentic, radical, outrageous, and divinely inspired. It is to be *you*—in your full, glorious power of blissful being!"

— **Kara Maria Ananda**, Healing Arts Educator and Social Business Coach

"Enlightenment occurs the second you realize darkness doesn't exist because of a lack of light; it exists because you haven't travelled far enough through it to discover you are the light."

— **Robert Clancy**, Author and Inspirational Speaker

"It's not about the opinions of others; it's about your opinion of you. Listen to your heart and take those risks. Believe in your learning process and be faithfully guided into your destiny."

— **Jenny Tasker**, Founder, Jenny's Positive Posts

"The Mona Lisa wasn't his masterpiece—Leonardo da Vinci was."

— **Corey Teramana**, Founder of The 9-to-5 Exit Plan

"The one thing all famous authors, world class athletes, business tycoons, singers, actors, and celebrated achievers in any field have in common is that they all began their journeys when they were none of these things."

— **Mike Dooley**, Author of *Notes from the Universe*

"As we walk the journey to integrate our enlightened being in our human form, we begin to cross the bridge that will bring us to discover our true divine essence. It is not a path of perfection; it is a path of devotion and commitment to the self."

— **Monica Jones**, Founder, From Loss to Love

"The moment you realize how magnificent you are by being just a unique human, [that] is the moment when the change starts. The entire universe is in your heart. To expand the universe, expand your heart."

— **Catherine B. Roy,** Founder, Live From Your Heart and Mind

"Move one pebble on the beach, and you change history."

— **Don Shapiro**, Founder, The Leadership Initiative

"In the end, it won't be about money, material possessions, fame, or beauty. It's always been about love. It's always been about living, not just being alive. It's always been and always will be about greeting every new sunrise with awe and every new sunset with gratitude."

— **Sheri Eckert**, Co-Founder and Program Director, Innerwork Portland

"Healing is similar to learning how to walk: it's a step-by-step process that takes time, effort, and focus."

— **Heather Durling**, Founder, Owner, and Practitioner, The Phoenix Gathering

"We speak of the great journey, which is life. We mourn the great journey, which is death. We feel with every breath the beauty of our existence. Take a breath; be present in your life now. Let each day be your journey."

— **Dru Ann Welch**, Owner of Readings, Healing, and Life Coaching by Dru Ann

"Honor the process, and the process will honor you."

— **David Wright**, Paradigm Performance Group

"We are here for only a moment in time. Spend your journey discovering all the wonderful souls who surround you—and spread love, peace, and your authentic crazy self to the world."

— **Valerie Ann Pizana**, Entrepreneur

"Never forget: your struggles are not greater than the power inside of you."

— **Tina Dill Tappy**, Social Media Manager, Died By Suicide

"Gratitude is happiness in seed form."

— **Sue Parry-Jones** Creator, Miles away from Abuse

"Success isn't just about what you accomplish in your life; it's about what you inspire others to do."

— **Beth Bracaglia**, Chief Simplicity Officer, Simply Organized

"When we allow ourselves to feel, when we become entirely willing to deal—it is at that moment we begin to heal."

— **Ashley Brewer**, Owner and Founder, Parents in Recovery

"You are the light that brightens this universe. Remember, inspiration starts with an *I*."

— **Anurag Singh**, Founder, Random Words of Kindness

"Something beautiful is wanting to blossom through you. Nurture that unique something at your core and let its magic be a gift of goodness to the universe that gives so much to you."

— **Gerry Straatemeier**, Writer, Mystic, and Happiness Coach

"May your gifts serve the world and bring you abundance and vibrant health."

— **Tyhson Banighen**, Intuitive Business Mentor

"I firmly believe that the journey *is* the destination!"

— **Corey Poirier**, TEDx Speaker, Top-Rated Radio Show Host, Bestselling Author

"When you may stay still in one place within, whilst going in and out of these worldly adventures spontaneously, you have achieved enlightenment."

— **Vishal Singh**, Co-Founder and Owner, The Purple Bridge

"Find the person who will ask, 'What happened to you?' and is careful with your mind, heart, and spirit. This person will guide you out of the darkness into the light."

— **Jacqueline Conroy**, Owner and Founder,
Jacqueline Conroy Talking Therapies

"Your problems don't define you; they are just part of your story."

— **Aimee Halpin**, Wellness Coach, Vitalize You

"Within you is an infinite universe of wisdom, love, and energy waiting for you to access it. Once you have tapped into it, you can bring yourself into a state of wellness and balance, discovering your authenticity, soul gifts, and true purpose. This transformation leads to your personal enlightenment, allowing you to live your real-life mission."

— **Heather Corinne Lang**, Owner, Namaste Rays

"Many times through self-examination you'll answer more than half the questions you normally look to others for."

— **Malcolm Bowen**, Entertainment Industry Professional

"My wish for you is that the light of your soul fills you so completely that you desire for nothing because you realize you already are and have everything!"

— **Shari Alyse**, Co-Founder and Owner, Soul Ventures Corp

"When we each accept and take full responsibility for our lives and ourselves, we see there are no mistakes, only lessons, that there is nothing to forgive and no one to blame."

— **Cheryl O'Connor**, Owner and Creator, Cheoco Enterprises

"Don't flee from negative thoughts or feelings; embrace them as if they are your children needing care, attention, and love. Embracing 'what is' gives you permission to be fully human and, in doing so, awakens a natural ability to love and accept yourself."

— **Kelly Martin**

"Perhaps the most difficult things that happen to you in life serve the purpose of pushing you deeper into yourself where you will discover what a magnificent spiritual being you really are."

— **Renae Sauter**, Owner, Create-Fate Enterprises

"We have all heard the famous quote, 'Life is short.' Keep in mind that life could be 'long' for you. Therefore, design a life that stands the test of time. Strive to be here for a good time *and* a long time!"

— **Jeff Winship**, Financial Security Advisor, Winship Wealth Group

"Relationships are like muscle tissue: the more they are engaged, the stronger and more valuable they become."

— **Ted Rubin**, Speaker and Author

"Above all, be kind to yourself and others."

— **Suzie Daggett**, Owner, Dear Source

"And this is the greatest thing of all: to truly accept and embrace oneself, wholly."
— **Holly Ruttenbur Dickinson**, Author, Homemaker, and Philanthropist

"When we see the beauty of God in every face, hate will vanish from this earth."
— **Barbara Pryor-Smith**, Owner, Oneness Happens Here

"Don't worry about how tough the journey would be; the moment you get there, you will forget and enjoy the view."

— **Batoul Aboutaam**

"Enlightened living is about being fully present. It is about remembering that you are already perfect, whole, and complete and that everything that happens in your life is an invitation to fall awake and beneath the busy mind into the deep peace, beauty, wisdom, and stillness that you have always been."

— **Kimberley Jones**, Entrepreneur

"Nothing I do, nothing I have done, and nothing that has been done to me impacts my worth—or yours. When we stop striving to be loved, that's when we find out how much we already are."

— **Christine Morgan**, Coach, 3-word Wisdom

"If your dreams are 'unreasonable,' you are on the right path. Be unstoppable."

— **Michael Currie**, The Fort Nova Group Ltd.

"If we do the right thing today, tomorrow we don't have to worry about having done something wrong."

— **Felicia Reed**, Founder and Owner, Put It In Perspective

"Respect, appreciate, and love yourself for what you are. Know that you are always complete the way you are, as you cannot be what you are not."

— **Helena Kalivoda**, Writer and Author

"True wellness is not necessarily the absence of disease or illness but how we handle life's challenges and function each day, with full alignment of body, mind, and soul."

— **Linda Gillan**, Founder and Owner, Heart of Linda

"Open your eyes each morning with a renewed spirit. In that moment, experience the joy, passion, gratitude, and excitement you feel knowing that you get to live yet another glorious day in your divine purpose."

— **Cathy Alves Davis**, Author of *Myrcles*

"When we understand the principle behind 'what we think about comes about,' we quickly understand the value of starting each day with an affirmation, a declaration setting the day in the direction we choose. 'Good morning, it is a great day' is what I tell the universe each and every morning."

— **Yittah Lawrence**, Founder and Owner,
Good Morning, It Is a Great Day

"When it comes down to it, we must feel our own joy, self-worth, and love. We can look for it everywhere—and in everyone and everything—but we will not find it anywhere but in our own hearts."

— **Jill Alman-Bernstein**, Author of *I Must Be A Mermaid*

"Taking an emotional holiday is just as important as taking a physical one. Allow yourself some time away. Make time to just *be*."

— **Teresa Walker**

"This dimension = the breadth of any event transpiring before us; it is only a reflection of the level of self that sees it. Unity doesn't mean uniformity."

— **JoAnn Aparo Neurath**, Founder of Saltcoats, Writer, and Photographer

"Pain is in your head. If you can create it, you can also destroy it, but it starts in your head."

— **Isaiah Jackson**, Marketer, Young Entrepreneur

"Fear will hold us back as long as we let it. So, what if instead of letting fear hold us back, we let it give us permission to move forward? When we learn to embrace fear, we learn to break through it, and on the other side of that fear is our opportunity to make an impact through the work we do."

— **Kate Erickson**, Entrepreneur and Podcaster

"I must remember to be myself and not get caught up in me, because myself, I am, but me, well that's another story!"

— **Imraan Omar**, Author, *The Arabic Quran: A Journey into Consciousness*

"Life is a circle, energy in constant motion. It goes out; it comes back. Giving of oneself, in whatever way we can, is just one part of the equation. We must also learn to receive."

— **Genie Lee Perron**, Life Coach, Artist, and Author

"Making friends with death starts with making friends with life. There is only one way off this planet, but while we are here, it's our right and duty to thrive!"

— **Catherine Whelan Costen**, Public Speaker and Clarity Coach

"When you have a rough day or are going through tough times, you are only allowed one day of wallowing in self-pity. That's it. One day! Tomorrow, you pick up and move on and deal—and always with a smile on your face."

— **Sabrina Powers**, Simulation Events Inc.

"When was the last time you used your magic to create your life? What if you were reminded of your own unique gifts and capacities? Just imagine the life of infinite possibility you could create beyond your dreams. Let's ignite that magic within! Is now the time?"

— **Tanya Desaulniers**, Access Bar Consciousness Facilitator,
"Being the Instrument of Magic

"If you wait until your house is on fire to buy your fire insurance, that fire insurance suddenly becomes very expensive. Please don't risk your life and health insurance premiums by waiting too long. We all have a 'best-before' date, and an excellent advisor should be able to help walk you through a comprehensive risk management process so as to ensure that you are insured and protected from all of the bumps along the road of life."

— **Jason Desaulniers** , Financial Advisor,
Excalibur Executive Planning Inc.

"You have to be a leader in your own life before you can ever lead other people."

— **Sharon Worsley**, Business Development Ninja,
Sharon Worsley International

"You can't hold someone's hand without your hand being held."

— **Teal Swan**, The Spiritual Catalyst

"Gratitude is not hard; it is so much like appreciation. It is done on purpose, can be done anytime and with a smile. It can be overly done or be only a second thought, here and there. It is essential to feel your way through appreciation, then appreciate, and vice versa. Same is true for gratitude; it is an attitude, not a concept."

— **Tamara Thompson**, Inspirational Self-Help Author
and Advocate for Children and Teens

"Achievers make defeat a learning process of success."

— **S. A. Jainul Abdeen**

"Emotions do not happen to us; emotions happen for us. There are no good or bad emotions. Rather, each emotion we feel carries important instinctive and intuitive information designed to help us navigate life with confidence and success. We simply need to learn how to listen to and understand our emotions to make them work for us, instead of feeling uncomfortable with or overwhelmed by them. That is the key to unlocking this powerful resource within."

— **Christy E Gray**, PhD Candidate, TEDx Speaker, and Relationship
Expert

"It's two things that children never forget: they never forget when someone is extremely kind to them or when someone is extremely mean to them."

— **Carolyn Denise Owens**, Author and Writer

"What if you were brought up to believe that you already are everything you think you need to grow up to be and that when you follow your passion and joy, you become a grander version of you? How would you feel about you now? Guess what? You already are everything you think you need to grow up to be! How do you like you now?"

— **Ilyse Rothman**, EFT Wellness Practitioner

"Land can be divided, but not love, as it was always equal for everyone."
— **Vipen Goswami**, Vipen Personified

"Believing is the first step to achieving."
— **Traci Johnstone**, Coauthor of *The Dangers of Depo, the World's Most Dangerous Birth Control*

"The human body's harmonious inner workings with the capacity to self-heal is awe-inspiring. In progressing to health, grasp the big picture, seek wisdom, and take personal responsibility to engage the right combination of intelligent, supportive therapies."
— **Susanne Morrone**, Consultant to Aspiring Health Champions

"Write your feelings down on paper—anything and everything that you are feeling. It helps not to be carrying all of those burdens around on your shoulders every day. Each day has enough of its own troubles."
— **Lorraine Price**, Author

"When you open your eyes to the possibility, only then can you see the vision."
— **Karen D. Brown**, Entrepreneur and Independent Contractor

"You can't control what happens around you, but you can control the way you tell your story, with or without the drama. It's up to you."
— **Michelle Bateman**, Marketing Manager

"There is a significant difference between doing nothing and not doing."
— **Ronald Keulen**, Masters in Science

"Life is like a sandwich; the more you add to it, the better it gets!"
— **Mark Morbeck**, Co-Owner and Positive Motivational Speaker, Positive Sandwich Plus

"As a chubby, awkward child, I was easily hurt by the name-calling and jokes aimed at me. All the cool kids ignored me. As I got older, I realized that I had something much better and an ally I never knew I had. I had ambition, intelligence, and a powerful desire to make my dreams come true. Now at fifty-three, I realize that by visualizing my future, I was creating it, and my sheer determination was the most important factor in creating my success. I never gave up because I always thought that success was just around the corner, and I would miss my chance if I did. And it always was—it was the Law of Attraction at work, my invisible ally. When I share this with others, they tell me I am crazy, so I ask them, 'How happy are you with your life now?' I'd rather be crazy!"

— **Lori Karpman**, CEO, Lori Karpman & Associates Ltd.

"Some people will think you walk on water no matter what you do; some people will hate you no matter what you do. It's how you handle the majority in the middle that determines your level of success."

— **Brian K. Wright**, Brian K Wright International

"You can have the most successful business in the world, but if you don't have your health, you might as well be bankrupt."

— **Carol Boyce**, Health Creator

"What's the secret to good health? Make it your priority."

— **Lucia Williams**, Wellness Coach

"A spark of remembrance of who I am, enhanced by the connection to the source of all that is, I embrace the new me that always was, as my understanding of my soul's journey awakens from within."

— **Ellen Carey**

"There's no standard template for life's issues. You have to create yours—in real time—as you walk along the path of life."

— **Ibiyemi Ifaturoti**, HR Consultant

"Be uncommon. Be yourself."

— **Lisa Mellinger**, Life Support Member

"Every day, you should do three things: something for yourself, something for someone else, and something that needs doing. First, you are special, unique, and God's creation—take time to read, learn, eat a great meal, listen to great music, whatever drives the uniqueness in you. Second, you are part of a mosaic of other unique individuals, and you can and should have a positive impact on them in some way, small or large—open a door for a lady, show kindness to someone in need, donate your time to a great cause. Finally, don't put off until tomorrow something that needs to be done today—take care of tasks and 'to do' lists and accomplish at least one positive thing every day."

— **Brad Raney**, Personal Performance Partnership

"Say what you mean; mean what you say."

— **Chris Rogers**

"I love working toward making a positive financial difference in people's lives and seeing them progress toward their goals and dreams. The side effect—I make a living by following my passion in helping others."

— **Marlene Simmons**, Financial Security Advisor, Investment Representative, and Elder Planning Counselor

"Surround yourself with beautiful things. Say yes to opportunity. Imagine the life you want and live it. Let creativity rule your world. Create your brilliance."

— **T. R. Sebastien**, Writer, Author of *The WindFinder*, and Motivational Blogger

"Wealth is a mindset, not the physical proof."

— **Tammy Braswell**, Energetic Creation Visionary

"It's gonna be a great day. I woke up, and right here, right now, I have everything I need. The rest of the day is a bonus. I am grateful. The great thing about this is that I do say this every day, and it puts the day into motion."

— **Don Kennedy**, Actor

"My belief is quite simple. It's not what I'm going to do for you that matters. What matters is, does what I do really work?"

— **Bob Angus**, Retired Real Estate Agent

"Don't confuse discernment with cynicism. Cynicism is discernment's lazy brother."

— **Audrey Gaddess**, Sales Team Leader

"We come alive when we share our passions. Doing so is a tremendous opportunity to do something that we love to do. They [passions] can change from moment to moment. Passion evolves with life."

— **Don Miguel Ruiz Jr.**, Author, *The Five Levels of Attachment*

"Sometimes you can achieve your life's goals by taking seemingly unrelated action. It's easy for me to do ten thousand steps a day to keep healthy. All I have to do is search for my keys."

— **Greg Gazin**, The Gadget Guy

"The thing I love most about working with successful business owners on Facebook is sharing their aha moments. When someone feels enlightened for the first time, they become empowered for life!"

— **Fiona MacNeil**, Social Media Strategist

"In the ordinary course of daily living and working, we are always dealing with perspectives that differ from our own. The grand paradox of being human is we are universally the same and individually unique. To 'QuantumThink' is to look from the whole. How can we ever see clearly if we cannot be with divergent points of view and ideas? If you cannot let another's perspective into your world, even for a moment of consideration, how can you begin to approach any kind of mastery?"

— **Dianne Collins**, Creator of QuantumThink
and Authority in New World View Thinking

"Almost every successful person that has been on my show, they have this in common: they have taken their story of personal tragedy to triumph and have turned it into their career, and then, they have used their career as a way to give back."

— **Lisa Garr Founder**, The Aware Show

"Most people who just chase the money end up having miserable lives because they end up doing things that they are not good at and are not passionate about. Instead, find out what you're really good at, and you will enjoy doing."

— **Rivers Corbett**, Entrepreneur, Speaker, and Startup Business Specialist

"Follow your dreams once you discover them. If it's not something you're passionate about or purpose driven for, don't do it. Instead, follow a passion, follow a purpose."

— **Mike Calderwood**, Coach, Mentor, and Advisor

"You may or may not realize it, but each person you come in contact with will impact your moment, your day, your decisions, and your life, so extend your positive attitude, perspective, or a simple smile. You are impacting the [lives] of those that come in contact with you."

— **Tiffany Hodgson**, Ron Hodgson GMC

"Every single human being on earth has within them an entrepreneur, a creator, an imagineer (as Walt Disney called them), and all we have to do is stimulate that individual using a process that we have invented. Someone will wake up in that person and be inspired to discover a passion that they never realized they had, or if they did realize they had it, they never believed that they could do it.

Suddenly, they are now face-to-face with themselves in this process and ready to build a system by which they take their mission out to the world."

— **Michael Gerber**, Co-Founder and Chairman,
Michael E. Gerber Companies, Creator, The E-Myth Evolution

"I'm learning how to let people help me. I love learning, and with all the new things I learn, I realize I can't do everything myself. I have to create community. Community comes in many forms—family, friends, clients, and other connections. I need help, and I'm learning how to let community help me. I used to do most things for myself, but I realized that was holding me back. I spent so much time doing the little things that needed done, I couldn't move forward. Now, I'm learning how to build a team to support my business. Love learning!"

— **Sandy Lawrence**, Perceptive PR

"Creativity without perspective is like faith without works."

— **Stan-The-HuMan**

"Follow your passion, and you will find your purpose."

— **Sherrill Rees**, CEO and Founder, Just Prevail

"1,440: the number that literally changes your life when you truly feel it. There are only 1,440 minutes in every day. Our minutes—time—is our most important asset. We can lose money, but make more. We can lose our health, but regain it. But time . . . tick, tick, tick . . . once it's gone, it's gone forever, and there are no guarantees we'll get more of it."

— **Kevin Kruse**, *New York Times* Bestselling Author

"Life, if we are lucky, has many chapters, with painful beginnings and endings. Change is never comfortable. There is always discomfort in birthing a new life."

— **Darlene MacInnis**, Consultant, Hypnotist,
Life Coach, and NLP Practitioner

"We need to learn to spend the same care and love decorating our inside homes as we do our material homes, and then fling the doors wide to welcome all."
— **Sue Marlene Woodworth-Scalia**, Medium and Aura Reader

"Taking action in adversity is the best tonic for fighting off the 'what if' and builds your empathetic story to teach and support others through. Who knew your most vulnerable moments could be your future lifeline?"
— **Holly Scott-Donaldson**, Editor and Publisher,
Back 2 Biz Magazine Founder, Action in Adversity Academy

"Change is best embraced with the mentality of, first, I crawl, then I walk, then I leap. Take every opportunity to embrace the process of change. One step in front of the other, one choice at a time creates sustainable change."
— **Kristy-Lea Tritz**, Heart-Centered Coach,
Bestselling Author, Speaker, and Trainer

"Being perfect is a state of mind. If we constantly strive to be perfect, we will never get there, but once we feel content with who we are, we will realize that we have been perfect all along."
— **Sandra Cooze**, Serafina Fae

"Be patient and wait for synchronicity to guide you. Listen to your intuition ("hunches") as this can lead to mysterious coincidences—the tiny miracles of opportunity that exist for every person. It's just that we don't always follow up on these coincidences, like meeting people at certain times, in elevators or the next table in a restaurant. If we did, we would find that we are guided at every moment into the knowledge and information we need to actualize ourselves and our dreams."
— **James Redfield**, Author of *The Celestine Prophecy*

"One of the most courageous things you can do is believe in yourself."
— **Elizabeth Kipp**

"You have to sell to help."

— **Marc Mawhinney**, Natural Born Coaches

"Never ever tell a child that they can't achieve what they want. I really feel strongly that it is a duty of an adult to push, encourage, and inspire our youth . . . if you ever have a chance to do that—that is a privilege. Never underestimate the impact you have on a child's life. People have absolutely no right to try and pull a child's dreams, hopes, and desires away. That is such a tragedy in my eyes. We live in a beautiful world where anything is possible, and they can have it if they want it badly enough and work hard enough for it. But they need to believe it. You as a role model should support that. There is a whole world of youth out there who need to be inspired. I want to be surrounded by enthusiasts, believers, and optimists . . . The world needs more of those kinds of people."

— **Nick Smyth**, Actor

"The chakra system is our inner diagnostic system, offering us deep wisdom and constant information about our health and well-being. We only need to tune into it to find the information to help bring us into balance."

— **Jenny Mannion**, Intuitive Healer

"Under the master's hand, what appears to the casual observer to be a broken thing is, in reality, something that is being transformed into a creature of greater value. For when all showiness is done away, all that is left is the true purpose of the master's creation."

— **Corina Delor**, Virtual Franchisee at Juice Plus+

"This may sound mean or unsympathetic, but one of my least favorite sayings is 'I gave my best.' To me, it is an unacceptable crutch. I don't want to hear it. My personal feeling is this: when the goal is to accomplish greatness, go where no one or team has gone before. I wasn't asking for your best effort; your best is what you were capable of in the past. I was expecting you to figure it out, to try a thousand ways and, if need be, try another thousand ways. I was expecting you to innovate, lose sleep, get around it, find loopholes, research, sweat like you never have before. Every extraordinary accomplishment, invention, or revolution was not a result of someone giving his or her best. Somehow that person or group found a way to do what no one else could do; they did the impossible; they did what no one had ever done before. The real issue is, it's not the effort that is in question at the moment or during the event; it's what you put into it leading up to it. Whether you win or lose, get the sale, ace the test, it is all determined by the effort given in preparing for the event. Every match is determined long before the contest happens. So, the next time you fail, before you want to make yourself feel better, saying, "I did my best," consider if you had given your best in preparation. The actual effort given in the event has the littlest to do with the outcome."

— **John R. DiJulius**, Bestselling Author of *The Customer Service Revolution*

"I thought I was doing everything right. Listened to all the motivational speakers. I read all the books, and I listened to the tapes, and nothing helped. Finally, I was very fortunate in that I went to a gentleman, who sort of dissed me to my father. He was extremely rich, and he simply said, 'Stop thinking what you're doing is right. Whatever you're doing isn't working, and you need to do something different.' I took that to heart. He also asked, 'What do you want to make your money in?' and I said business. He said, 'Are you the world's expert in business?' I said no, so he said, 'Well, until you are, don't come and talk to me again.' He said, 'Study rich people.' I've since discovered it's the who you are and it's the how you do it that matters."

— **T. Harv Eker**, Speaker and International
Bestselling Author of *Secrets of the Mind*

"They had a lot of determination to get their music across at the time. They were innovators. They revered Elvis because he opened the doors for them, but they were innovators in their own right. And focused—Mick Jagger was very focused on what he was doing. Very smart, clever, and he used his intense sexuality to entice people to buy his music. There really are so many variables as to why certain people achieved a high level of success in the music industry, but at the end of the day, they really just wanted to get their music out into the world—into people's ears and hearts and souls."

— **Pamela Des Barres**, Former Rock and Roll Groupie,
Author of *I'm with the Band and Take Another Little Piece of
My Heart,* Former Member of the All-Girl Group The GTOs

"In terms of shortcuts to reaching the top level, I would say surround yourself with the right people and find good mentors, both from inside and outside of your industry, who have been where you need to go, and learn from their experience. To me, no matter what industry you're in, that is a great approach to take. Keep in mind that sometimes a mentor can be a one-off situation, and other times it can be ongoing. A good way to accomplish this or ensure this happens is to join associations where those mentors are sure to be and make sure to get engaged with the association or group."

— **Mark Black**, Speaker, Bestselling Author

"People write books about (passion) all the time, like *The Secret*. You have to believe it to achieve it. It's even in the Bible—it is done unto you as you believe, but that's always been true, I feel. People sort of handicap themselves by putting a time limit on things, and then if they don't do it, they throw in the towel. I didn't care how long it took. I was just going to keep my eyes on the prize. If you just take one step after another, you'll be surprised how fast things actually happen. The best part is, taking one step forward toward your goal is always better than standing still."

— **Patti Johnsen**, Former Rock and Roll Groupie,
Founder of the Groupie Round Table

"Sometimes the biggest risk is taking none at all. I was terrified of failure, so very hesitant to take any chance unless I was sure I could succeed. What was I so afraid of? Consider this: we all know our time here on earth is temporary. The 'risks' we weigh in life or in business are rarely life-threatening. In fact, when we really consider the absolute worst-case scenario, it's not as bad as we make it out to be. If things don't go well, we may have a bruised ego, but we'll probably still have our family and friends and a roof over our head. And on the flip side, if things do go well, the results could be life-changing in a big, positive way."

— **Nick Loper**, The Side Hustle Brand

"When we percolate, we gradually improve ourselves and others as our message we share with the world expands. When we are our best self, we touch the lives and hearts of others in positive, compassionate, and often enlightening ways. To begin percolating and being our best, we must first understand that our life opens up when we shift our energy into our passions and talents that tap into our soul. This—combined with developing and using your own set values, goals, and a belief and behavior system—will support the lifestyle changes you wish to make to brew your best life. You go where you place your energy."

— **Elizabeth Hamilton-Guarino**, Hay House
Author and Founder of the Best Ever You Network

"The superstars are a step above anyone else. We are all playing in the National Hockey League (NHL) and couldn't play any higher than we were at, yet we would all marvel at the things Mario could do or the things that Paul Coffee could do. Their mindset was different in that they never had the self-doubt that others, even in the NHL, might have."

— **Rob Brown**, Former Pittsburg Penguin Forward

"If you walk around with a smile on your face, others smile. If you walk around with a frown, others frown. Why would you want to leave people worse off than found them?"

— **Jimmy Flynn**, Musical Comedian

"Try to sell something before you start building it. You want to make sure people want it before you spend years building it. The biggest mistake a lot of entrepreneurs make is they spend years building something nobody wants. You also have to be passionate about what you're selling. If you're passionate about it, you'll find a way to sell it. If you're not, it's just a grind, and it never works out."

— **Nick Nanton**, CEO, Dicks & Nanton Companies

"Following our dreams and living out our visions can sometimes feel as if a commitment to our authentic selves is a lonely journey, yet the very real truth is, there is never a crowd on the leading edge."

— **Catherine E. Arsenault**, Founder, PEI Local

"You were born to be real, not to be perfect."

— **Demo Casanova**, Life Strategist, Creative Director

"Life is memories in motion, so breath in every moment like it's your last."

— **Shelley Rogerson**, Mission To Transition

CPSIA information can be obtained
at www.ICGtesting.com
Printed in the USA
LVHW092259280220
648594LV00001B/74